MW00423623

STRENGTH
FOR
THE
BATTLE

STRENGTH
FOR THE BATTLE

FRANCIS FRANGIPANE

CHARISMA
HOUSE

Most CHARISMA HOUSE BOOK GROUP products are available at special quantity discounts for bulk purchase for sales promotions, premiums, fund-raising, and educational needs. For details, write Charisma House Book Group, 600 Rinehart Road, Lake Mary, Florida 32746, or telephone (407) 333-0600.

STRENGTH FOR THE BATTLE by Francis Frangipane
Published by Charisma House
Charisma Media/Charisma House Book Group
600 Rinehart Road
Lake Mary, Florida 32746
www.charismahouse.com

Cover design by Vincent Pirozzi
Design Director: Justin Evans

Visit the author's website at www.frangipane.org.

Library of Congress Cataloging-in-Publication Data:
An application to register this book for cataloging has been
submitted to the Library of Congress.
International Standard Book Number: 978-1-62998-912-9
E-book ISBN: 978-1-62998-913-6

17 18 19 20 21 — 9 8 7 6 5 4 3 2 1
Printed in China

For though we walk in the flesh, we do not war according to the flesh. For the weapons of our warfare are not carnal, but mighty through God to the pulling down of strongholds, casting down imaginations and every high thing that exalts itself against the knowledge of God, bringing every thought into captivity to the obedience of Christ.
—2 CORINTHIANS 10:3–5

WISDOM BEFORE WARFARE,
VIRTUE BEFORE VICTORY

Wisdom is better than strength....
Wisdom is better than weapons of war.
—ECCLESIASTES 9:16, 18

JESUS PREPARED HIS disciples for everything, including war. They saw Him casting out demons. In fact, He sent them forth doing the same. But before He sent them out, He charged them to become wise "as serpents" yet innocent and harmless "as doves" (Matt. 10:16). This fusion of divine wisdom and Christlike innocence is the taproot of all spiritual victory. Indeed, we can defeat the enemy, but wisdom must precede warfare and virtue must come before victory. We must learn the ways of God, which means we must *think* with wisdom. And we must be pure of heart, that we may see God and gain discernment.

> *Almighty God, give me Your wisdom in all situations as You write on my heart what is true, honorable, right, pure, lovely, excellent, and worthy of praise that I might dwell on these things constantly as I contend by Your grace against evil and offer oppression no peace. Amen.*

MY SPIRITUAL PREPARATION FOR TODAY:

_____

_____

_____

_____

_____

AN ARMY OF REDEEMERS

*In whom you also are being built together into
a dwelling place of God through the Spirit.*
—EPHESIANS 2:22

I HAVE KNOWN, ON occasion, the intimidation of the prince of darkness. I've felt the weight of his confidence as he gloats at how unprepared the church is—how divided and carnal. He has no doubt that ultimately his kingdom will completely rule this world.

However, the immutable Word declares it will be the kingdom of the Most High that expands worldwide, not the kingdom of darkness. As it is written of God's kingdom, "Of [its] increase...there shall be no end" (Isa. 9:7).

Therefore let us not surrender to fear or unbelief. If Satan has legions of demons, God has an army of redeemers. In truth, as each of us matures, we must stop thinking of ourselves merely as "church people" and more as a society of redeemers, for that is what we become as we are conformed to the heart of Jesus Christ (Rom. 8:28–29).

> *O God, just as Jesus prayed that His disciples would be one, I pray that all believers everywhere will be united as one body so that the church, bound together by the power of Your love, may rise up in unity until darkness is fully overcome by the light, which is Jesus Christ. Amen!*

MY SPIRITUAL PREPARATION FOR TODAY:

_____

_____

_____

BE BOLD, NOT BRASH

*Every purpose is established by counsel,
and with good advice wage war.*
—PROVERBS 20:18

WE ALL HAVE seen many who have fallen. Jesus warned that the love of many would grow cold. Do not presume it cannot happen to you. Our enemy has been deceiving mankind for thousands of years. Our experience, on the other hand, spans but a brief moment. It is wisdom to recognize that we do not know all there is to know concerning warfare.

Therefore, be bold, but never brash or arrogant in your prayer life. Use your spiritual authority administratively, compassionately, but never presumptuously. Multitudes of well-meaning but ignorant Christians have approached the field of spiritual battle with flippant attitudes and have suffered greatly for it. Study and seek confirmation from the Lord for your strategies.

> *Gracious and loving heavenly Father, be my companion always. May I know You as You have revealed Yourself in the Scriptures. Daily illuminate my mind with Your wisdom. Strengthen me that I may stand on the day of battle, confident in the One who defeated all evil. Hallelujah! Amen.*

MY SPIRITUAL PREPARATION FOR TODAY:

_____

_____

_____

_____

_____

Arm Yourself With Discernment

Hatred stirs up strife, but love covers all sins.
—**Proverbs 10:12**

THERE ARE TIMES when I feel completely outraged by what the devil is doing to people, especially children. I burn inwardly with anger at the injustice and heartache I see in the world. But I know that my anger, by itself, cannot attain the righteousness of God (James 1:20). I must gather my passions and submit them to the Holy Spirit that they may regenerate into a redemptive response, even one that empowers my conformity to Christ.

Therefore let's arm ourselves with discernment and wisdom, and reach in faith to possess the mind of Christ. Jesus said, "This gospel of the kingdom will be preached throughout the world as a testimony to all nations, and then the end will come" (Matt. 24:14). The world has seen Christianity; let us now reveal Christ as He manifests Himself through a society of redeemers.

> *O Father, arm me with discernment and wisdom. Remind me afresh today that I am Your workmanship, created in Christ Jesus for good works, which You ordained that I should walk in. Let all that I do be done in love, the mightiest weapon in Heaven and on earth. Amen.*

MY SPIRITUAL PREPARATION FOR TODAY:

_____

_____

_____

_____

RELIGIOUS SELF-DECEPTION

*Therefore guard your minds, be sober, and hope
to the end for the grace that is to be brought
to you at the revelation of Jesus Christ.*
—1 PETER 1:13

MANY BELIEVERS HAVE been taught that, because they have the Holy Spirit, they cannot be deceived. This is untrue. One reason the Spirit of Truth was sent was because we so easily fall into self-deception. In fact, the very thought that a Christian cannot be deceived is itself a deception! Once a particular lie permeates a believer's mind, his ideas and opinions crystallize and remain in whatever state of spiritual immaturity he happens to be. All manner of spirits will attack the soul, knowing they are protected by the armor of that person's own thoughts and doctrines.

You may not agree with the idea that evil spirits can frequent and occupy attitudes in a believer's life, but you must certainly agree that each of us has a carnal mind that is a source of vain imaginations and thoughts that exalt themselves above God. We deal with the devil by dealing with the carnal thought systems, the strongholds, that protect the enemy.

> *O Lord, in the power of Your Spirit let my natural mind be overtaken by Your holy mind. Put a right spirit within me that chafes at deception and cringes at lies. Cleanse my thoughts, cleanse my heart, and lead me in Your ways everlasting! Amen.*

MY SPIRITUAL PREPARATION FOR TODAY:

_____

_____

THE BATTLEGROUND OF THE MIND

*He has delivered us from the power of darkness and
has transferred us into the kingdom of His dear Son.*
—COLOSSIANS 1:13

YOU WILL REMEMBER that the location where Jesus was crucified was called *Golgotha*, which means "place of the skull."
If we will be effective in spiritual warfare, the first field of conflict where we must learn warfare is the battleground of the
mind; i.e., the "place of the skull." Indeed, the territory of the
uncrucified thought life is the beachhead of satanic assault in
our lives. To defeat the devil, we must be crucified in the place
of the skull. We must be renewed in the spirit of our minds!

> *Gracious Father, You have called me out of dark-
> ness into Your marvelous light, and for this I give
> You thanks and praise! Please continually crucify
> my "old man" that I might be born afresh of Your
> Spirit, always and in everything, to the glory of Your
> name! Amen.*

MY SPIRITUAL PREPARATION FOR TODAY:

_____

_____

_____

_____

_____

_____

_____

THE REAL ANTICHRIST SPIRIT

*Seek the LORD while He may be found, call
you upon Him while He is near.*
—ISAIAH 55:6

FOLLOWING CHRIST CALLS us to embrace forgiveness and love as a way of life. It is simply "anti" Christ to justify unforgiveness, division, and selfish ambition. *The antichrist spirit will be disguised behind any number of issues, but those issues are simply tools this principality uses to divide the church.*

The spirit of antichrist is simply that spirit which is anti-Christ. It is anti-love, anti-forgiveness, anti-reconciliation. Perhaps more than all others, this principality keeps good churches divided from one another.

The antichrist spirit may use jealousy or fear or even the color of the church bathrooms as a smoke screen, but the essential cause of most division is simply Christians yielding to someone or something other than the Spirit and teachings of Jesus Christ.

Any situation can be reconciled by returning to the words of Jesus. Once all parties yield to Him, love and victory soon follow.

> *Dear Lord, guard my heart from unforgiveness, jealousy, fear, and criticism so that I do not open doors for this divisive spirit to enter and cause destruction. Amen.*

MY SPIRITUAL PREPARATION FOR TODAY:

_____

_____

_____

_____

DAY 8

BECAUSE HE LIVES IN US

But he who is joined to the Lord becomes one spirit with Him.
—1 CORINTHIANS 6:17

As WE LEARN to think as a redeemer, we will increasingly find our thoughts being synchronized with the mind of Christ. One may argue that no mere man or woman who has been a sinner can become a redeemer. I agree; we cannot pay the full price for someone's redemption. To think otherwise is to blaspheme. At the same time, there is not a different Jesus in us than mankind's Redeemer who ascended into Heaven; Christ is the Redeemer seated in Heaven and He is the Redeemer seated in us.

If we are true sheep, we will begin to discern His voice. We will see evidences of His protection and healing that we never recognized before. Just as we become holy because He is holy (1 Pet. 1:16), so we become redeemers because He is the Redeemer.

> *Dear Jesus, God's truth made flesh, come and take up residence in my heart now and always. Give me a fresh awareness of Your mercies. Let the fire of Your love consume me until all of You overtakes all of me. Blessed be Your name! Amen.*

MY SPIRITUAL PREPARATION FOR TODAY:

DISCERNING YOUR OWN DARKNESS

Take heed therefore lest the light which is in you is darkness.
—LUKE 11:35

FOR MOST, THE term *spiritual warfare* introduces a new, but not necessarily welcome, dimension in their Christian experience. The thought of facing evil spirits in battle is an unsettling concept, especially since we came to Jesus as lost sheep, not warriors. Ultimately some of us may never actually initiate spiritual warfare, but all of us must face the fact that the devil has initiated warfare against us. Therefore it is essential to our basic well-being that we discern the areas of our nature that are unguarded and open to satanic assault.

Let us recognize, before we do warfare, that the areas we hide in darkness are the very areas of our future defeat. Often the battles we face will not cease until we discover and repent for the darkness that is within us. If we will be effective in spiritual warfare, we must be discerning of our own hearts; we must walk humbly with our God.

> *O Father, take my heart and let it be consecrated to You that I might walk in Your light. As Your Word says in Psalm 139:23–24, I ask You to "search me, O God, and know my heart; try me, and know my concerns, and see if there is any rebellious way in me, and lead me in the ancient way." Amen.*

MY SPIRITUAL PREPARATION FOR TODAY:

_____

_____

_____

DAY 10

NEARNESS TO CHRIST

But it is good for me to draw near to God; I have taken my refuge in the Lord GOD, that I may declare all Your works.
—PSALM 73:28

IT IS OUR nearness to Christ that produces virtue, healing gifts, and spiritual discernment. As Jesus promised: "He who believes in Me will do the works that I do also" (John 14:12).

We generally assume the Lord was referring to miracles when He said we would accomplish the works that He did. However, while miracles are part of the overall works of Christ, Jesus did not limit His definition of *works* to the miraculous. The works He did were diverse and many: He lived a redemptive life, He spent nights in prayer, He forgave His persecutors, He identified with the poor and needy, He rendered Himself as a guilt offering for mankind's sins, and so on. If Christ truly becomes our life, then *all* the works that He did, we "will do also," and this includes what I refer to as possessing the mind of Christ. True Christians are the progeny of Christ.

> *Precious Jesus, draw my heart close to Your heart today. Fill my imagination with Your love. And if I should begin to wander even just a little from You, call me back quickly and tenderly. I love You. Thank You for loving me. Amen.*

MY SPIRITUAL PREPARATION FOR TODAY:

_____

_____

_____

_____

THE TIME OF THRESHING

Then the Lord said, "Simon, Simon, listen! Satan
has demanded to have you to sift you as wheat."
—LUKE 22:31

SATAN WILL NEVER be given permission to destroy the saints. Rather, he is limited to sifting them "as wheat."

There is wheat inside each one of us. Our husk-like outer nature must die to facilitate the breaking forth of the wheat-like nature of the new creation man. Both the chaff and the husk were necessary; they provided protection for us from the harsh elements of this life. But before God can truly use us, in one way or another, we will pass through a time of threshing.

Dear Father God, though I would try and run from
the fire of Your sifting, when it comes, let my faith
not fail me. Though Satan desires me, I know You
desire me more. Precious Jesus, pray for me in my
time of trial just as You prayed for Peter, that I may
emerge on the other side to find Your arms waiting
for me. Amen.

MY SPIRITUAL PREPARATION FOR TODAY:

_____

_____

_____

_____

_____

_____

_____

WHAT WE MUST AVOID

For all have sinned and come short of the glory of God.
—ROMANS 3:23

A S A SOCIETY of redeemers, we must flee from loveless attitudes, especially the Pharisaic attitude of those who trust
in themselves that they are righteous while viewing others with
contempt (Luke 18:9–14). In spite of the conflicts in our world
and regardless of the ever-accelerating advance of hell, we do
not abandon our role to serve God's redemptive purposes.

I am not saying we shouldn't cry out against evil. However,
at some point we must recognize there is more to our destiny
than judging sin in other people. God is looking for the perfection of mercy within us; "mercy triumphs over judgment"
(James 2:13). May the world see Jesus manifest through us.

> *Dear Lord, I invite You to build Your kingdom in
> my heart today. Make me worthy by Your unlim-
> ited gift of grace to tell of Your love to everyone I
> encounter regardless of their situation. Let me see
> each person through the lens of Your love. Amen.*

MY SPIRITUAL PREPARATION FOR TODAY:

_____

_____

_____

_____

_____

_____

_____

IT TAKES A "JEHU" TO CONQUER JEZEBEL

When Jehu came to Jezreel, Jezebel heard about it. She put
black paint on her eyes, adorned her head, and looked down
through the window. As Jehu entered in at the gate...they
dropped her down and some of her blood splattered on
the wall and on the horses. Then he trampled her.
—2 KINGS 9:30–33

THERE WAS SOMETHING in Jehu's spirit that we must possess today. While we must be compassionate toward those
captured by Jezebel's influence (see Revelation 2:21), we must
show no mercy to the Jezebel spirit itself. Jehu offered Jezebel
no hope for reform, no compromise whatsoever.

So we must offer this demon no opportunity to probe our
soul and unlock vulnerabilities to her "many witchcrafts." She
must be cast down from her high place of influence. Indeed, as
she lay bleeding and near death, Jehu "trampled her!" Likewise
we must follow Christ and fearlessly walk upon this serpent,
crushing it under our feet. (See Luke 10:19; Romans 16:20.)

> *Father! I have need of You! When I encounter the*
> *spirit of Jezebel, let that same spirit that was in Jehu*
> *rise up in me and offer no mercy, no tolerance, and*
> *no compromise. Teach me how to have compassion*
> *for those under this spirit's influence while I cast her*
> *down and side with God to see her conquered. In*
> *the mighty name of Jesus I pray, amen.*

MY SPIRITUAL PREPARATION FOR TODAY:

_____

_____

_____

AN HONEST HEART

*But He gives more grace. For this reason it says: "God
resists the proud, but gives grace to the humble."*
—JAMES 4:6

Do you know the areas where you are vulnerable to satanic assault? Jesus would have us not be ignorant of our need. In fact, when He reveals the sin in our hearts, it is so He might destroy the works of the devil. Thus we should realize that *the greatest defense we can have against the devil is to maintain an honest heart before God.*

When the Holy Spirit shows us an area that needs repentance, we must overcome the instinct to defend ourselves. We must silence the little lawyer who steps out from a dark closet in our minds, pleading, "My client is not so bad." Your "defense attorney" will defend you until the day you die—and if you listen to him, you will never see what is wrong in you or face what needs to change. For you to succeed in warfare, your self-preservation instincts must be submitted to the Lord Jesus, for Christ alone is your true advocate.

> *O God, establish my footsteps by Your Word. Do not let any iniquity have dominion over me. Your will be done in my life as it is in Heaven. Come and accomplish a mighty work in me to the glory of Your name. Amen.*

MY SPIRITUAL PREPARATION FOR TODAY:

_____

_____

_____

A Fellowship of Deliverers

Be therefore merciful, as your Father is merciful.
—Luke 6:36

In following Him, and through our union with Him, we become a fellowship of deliverers. We are not deliverers in the way Jesus delivered the world, but within the sphere of our limited environment—in our world of friends, family, and community—we exercise the same mentality as Christ: *we seek not to judge our world but to save it.*

Of course, along the way the enemy will seek to stop us. He will use offenses, slander, and persecution. However, as Christ followers, when wounded, we forgive; when forced to go one mile, we go two. We bless those who curse us and turn the other cheek to those who strike us.

Lamb of God, replace my judgment with Your mercy. Teach me how to forgive. Show me what it means to be Your light in my world. Strengthen me in all goodness by the power of Your Holy Spirit today. Amen.

My spiritual preparation for today:

_____

_____

_____

_____

_____

_____

_____

DAY 16

JESUS IN YOUR HEART

*Know the God of your fathers and serve Him
with a whole heart and with a willing spirit.*
—1 CHRONICLES 4:23

VICTORY BEGINS WITH the name of Jesus on your lips, but it will not be consummated until the nature of Jesus is in your heart. This rule applies to every facet of spiritual warfare. Indeed, Satan will be allowed to come against the area of your weakness until you realize God's only answer is to become Christlike. As you begin to appropriate not just the name of Jesus but His nature as well, the adversary will withdraw. Satan will not continue to assault you if the circumstances he designed to destroy you are now working to perfect you.

Indeed, it is of the greatest truth that once the devil recognizes his assault against your life has not pulled you from God but toward Him—once he perceives that his temptations are actually forcing you to appropriate the virtue of Christ—the enemy will withdraw.

> *Dear Lord, show me what I must do so that the darkness in me is displaced by Your nature in my heart. Teach me what it means to be humble and contrite in spirit. I long to become more fully Christlike. Take me by the hand, precious Lord, and lead me. Amen.*

MY SPIRITUAL PREPARATION FOR TODAY:

_____

_____

_____

_____

A Heart in Submission

Therefore submit yourselves to God. Resist
the devil, and he will flee from you.
—JAMES 4:7

JAMES 4:6 SAYS, "God resists the proud, but gives grace to the humble." Other translations say God "is opposed to" the proud. This is a very important verse. If God is opposed to the proud, and we are too proud to humble ourselves and admit when we are wrong, then God is opposed to us.

When we quote James 4:7, it is usually all by itself as a monument to spiritual warfare. However, it is in the context of repentance, humility, and possessing a clean heart (v. 6) that we find Satan fleeing from us.

We must go beyond a vague submission to God; we must submit the exact area of our personal battle to Him. When we come against the power of the devil, it must be from a heart in submission to Jesus.

> *O God, show me any area of my heart that is not in*
> *submission to You. Give me grace as I resist the urge*
> *to defend myself. I humble myself before You. Amen.*

MY SPIRITUAL PREPARATION FOR TODAY:

_____

_____

_____

_____

_____

_____

LEARNING TO WAIT AND
LISTEN TO THE LORD

He leads me in paths of righteousness for His name's sake.
—PSALM 23:3

WE MUST RELEARN how to think. We must learn how to pause before we speak—give ourselves a moment to enter the secret place of God's presence—and then listen to what Jesus has to say. For Christ Himself is the source of our discernment. In listening, we create the opportunity to hear the Lord's voice; postured before Him, we can receive answers, wisdom, and insights that we otherwise would not discern.

Indeed, using the gift of discernment, we can counter the advance of the enemy and reverse the gains he might have otherwise obtained.

> *O Father, help me in the heat of the moment to slip into the shelter of Your calming presence so that the enemy may find no foothold in my thoughts and actions. Set the ears of my heart forever on Your voice and Yours alone, that my life may always and everywhere give You glory. Amen.*

MY SPIRITUAL PREPARATION FOR TODAY:

_____

_____

_____

_____

_____

_____

HUMILITY: THE STRONGHOLD
OF THE LORD

*The sacrifices of God are a broken spirit; a broken
and contrite heart, O God, You will not despise.*
—PSALM 51:17

SATAN FEARS VIRTUE. He is terrified of humility; he hates it.
He sees a humble person, and it sends chills down his back.
His hair stands up when Christians kneel down, for humility is
the surrender of the soul to God. The devil trembles before the
meek because, in the very areas where he once had access, there
stands the Lord, and Satan is terrified of Jesus Christ.

> *O God, as I bend the knee of my heart to You, I am
> confident of Your gracious goodness toward me even
> while I am still a sinner. May You find me on my
> knees daily, surrendering my soul afresh to You, the
> Lord of Heaven and earth. Take me into that per-
> fect shelter of Your grace in Jesus Christ where I can
> look honestly at my sin and find it too objection-
> able to hold on to for even another minute. I thank
> You and praise You that Your mercies are new every
> morning! Amen.*

MY SPIRITUAL PREPARATION FOR TODAY:

_____

_____

_____

_____

_____

DAY 20

WHO ARE YOU TRULY FIGHTING?

You are dust.
—GENESIS 3:19

YOU WILL REMEMBER that, at the fall of man in the Garden of Eden, the judgment of God against the devil was that he should eat dust (Gen. 3:14). Remember also that God said of man, "You are dust" (v. 19). The essence of our carnal nature—of all that is carnal in nature—is dust. We need to see the connection here: Satan feeds upon our earthly, carnal nature of "dust." Satan dines on what we withhold from God.

Therefore we need to recognize that the immediate source of many of our problems and oppressions is not demonic but fleshly in nature. We must contend with the fact that one aspect of our lives, our flesh nature, will always be targeted by the devil. These fleshly areas supply Satan with a ready avenue of access to undermine our prayers and neutralize our walk with God.

> *O Father, I confess that so often Your humility is far from my heart. I know the dark places in my heart need the fire of Your presence to burn away the dross. Please reach deep into the innermost parts of me and replace any harshness, hatred, and list of grievances with Your love, hope, and forgiveness. Set a hedge of protection around me and fill me with Your beautiful truth, to the glory of Your name! Amen.*

MY SPIRITUAL PREPARATION FOR TODAY:

_____

_____

_____

THE LIVING VOICE OF JESUS

My sheep hear My voice, and I know them, and they follow Me.
—JOHN 10:27

WHEN WE ACCEPT Christ into our hearts, He does not enter simply as a doctrine. No, He enters us as a living voice. His Spirit brings conviction and direction; He speaks through dreams, visions, revelation, and understanding of the Scriptures. He illuminates our hearts, speaking to us of repentance and the renewal of our soul. He lifts us, reminding us of the faithful promises of God.

Yet this voice—the sacred voice of God—refuses to compete with the clamor of our fleshly minds. This is God, King and Creator of the universe. He requires the honor of our full attention! He will not yell as though we were disobedient children. He will not chase us. He waits.

Jesus taught, "Take heed what you hear" (Mark 4:24). Do we truly know how to listen? Discernment is the art of listening to Him who does not speak audibly and perceiving Him who is otherwise invisible.

> *Father, help me to be still before You so that You can renew me with Your presence. Tune my ears to Your voice until it becomes the one voice I hear above the clamor. Open the Scriptures afresh to me. Draw me closer. Amen.*

MY SPIRITUAL PREPARATION FOR TODAY:

_____

_____

_____

FIGHTING YOUR OWN REFLECTION

And those who are in the flesh cannot please God.
—ROMANS 8:8

BEFORE WE LAUNCH out in aggressive warfare, we must realize that many of our battles are merely the consequences of our own actions. Allow me to give you an example. My wife and I once lived in an area where a beautiful red cardinal kept its nest. Cardinals are very territorial and will fight off intruding cardinals zealously. At that time we owned a van that had large side mirrors and chrome bumpers. Occasionally the cardinal would attack the bumpers or mirrors, thinking his reflection was another bird. One day, as I watched the cardinal assail the mirror, I thought, "What a foolish creature; his enemy is merely the reflection of himself." Immediately the Lord spoke to my heart: "And so also are many of your enemies the reflection of yourself."

Before we have any strategy for attacking Satan, we must make sure that the real enemy is not our own carnal nature. We must ask ourselves, "Are the things oppressing me today the harvest of what I planted yesterday?"

> *Dear Father, take hold of me now that I may learn how to discern what is of the flesh and what is of the devil, so that I might reap in righteousness rather than slogging through fields of oppression. Thank You for loving me again today! Amen.*

MY SPIRITUAL PREPARATION FOR TODAY:

_____

_____

_____

YOUR BROTHER'S KEEPER

*The effective, fervent prayer of a
righteous man accomplishes much.*
—JAMES 5:16

WHEN THE ENEMY seeks to bring us to a place of contention or division with one or more people, we must discern this satanic activity as a plot to keep us all from a blessing that God intended for us. Thus we must turn quickly to intercession for that person or church.

This prayer posture must expand beyond our immediate church relationships into the citywide body of Christ. We are our brother's keeper. We must recognize that if we are to be effective in resisting the enemy, the church will have to become a house of prayer.

> *Lord, I ask You to grant me the gift of discernment. Forgive me for judging others and for failing to see the work of the enemy who seeks to divide us. Father, I submit to the mind of Christ; I ask for His perception so that I would have insight into what You are doing in the church. In Jesus's name, amen.*

MY SPIRITUAL PREPARATION FOR TODAY:

_____

_____

_____

_____

_____

_____

JESUS IS OUR RIGHTEOUSNESS

*Therefore, since we have been justified by faith, we
have peace with God through our Lord Jesus Christ.*
—ROMANS 5:1

SATAN, AS OUR adversary, stands as the accuser of the brethren
before God, the judge of all. The truth Christ wants us to see
is that when we approach God on the basis of our own righteousness, the adversary will always have legal grounds to cast
us into prison, for our righteousness is "as filthy rags" (Isa. 64:6).

Our salvation is not based upon what we do, but upon who
Jesus becomes to us. Christ Himself is our righteousness. We
have been justified by our faith; our peace with God comes
through our Lord Jesus Christ (Rom. 5:1). When Satan comes
against you, he tries to deceive you by focusing your attention
upon your own righteousness. The more we recognize that Jesus
alone is our righteousness, the less the adversary can assault us
in the arena of our failings.

> *Heavenly Father, I humbly come before You, guilty
> as charged. But I thank You for the righteousness of
> Jesus, my Savior and advocate. Cleanse me of any
> wrongdoing, and draw me closer to You today. I put
> no trust in human righteousness, but I lean fully on
> Jesus and the blood He shed on the cross for me. In
> His name I pray, amen.*

MY SPIRITUAL PREPARATION FOR TODAY:

_____

_____

_____

IN THE BRIGHTNESS OF HIS LOVE

Let us then come with confidence to the throne of grace, that we may obtain mercy and find grace to help in time of need.
—HEBREWS 4:16

WHEN THE ACCUSER comes seeking to condemn you for not having enough love, your response should be, "That is true; I do not have enough love. But the Son of God died for *all* my sins, even the sin of imperfect love." Step out from the shadow of satanic assault and stand in the brightness of your Father's love. Submit yourself to God and ask for Christ's love and forgiveness to replace your weak and imperfect love.

When Satan seeks to condemn you for impatience, again your response should be, "Yes, in my flesh I am very impatient. But since I have been born again, *Jesus* is my righteousness, and through His blood I am forgiven and cleansed." Turn again to God. Use the accusation as a reminder that you are not standing before an angry God but rather a throne of grace that enables you to boldly draw near to God for help. (See Hebrews 4:16.) The strength of humility is that it builds a spiritual defense around your soul, prohibiting strife, competition, and many of life's irritations from stealing your peace.

> *Father, I need the strength of Your humility in my life today. I need the brightness of Your love to overtake any and all attempts of the enemy to dislodge me from walking with You. Be the Lord of my life today. Amen.*

MY SPIRITUAL PREPARATION FOR TODAY:

_____

_____

Avoid Gossip

Let the words of my mouth and the meditation
of my heart be acceptable in Your sight, O
Lord, my strength and my Redeemer.
—Psalm 19:14

MANY PEOPLE THINK of witchcraft as coming against us from outside the body of Christ. However, there is another means through which Satan binds people with curses: misled Christians. Gossip and backbiting among Christians are primary gates through which curses and witchcraft gain access into the church.

Until the body of Christ learns to pray for one another, we will continually find ourselves being manipulated by demons. Consider this: the most common activity of Christians when they discover sin or failure is not to weep and pray but to descend into the darkness of gossip. Such unbridled talk brings what amounts to a curse against the individual who has stumbled. It ministers death—witchcraft under the influence of a religious spirit—that manifests in a tangible way, covering all involved like a shroud.

If you have a problem with a fellow Christian, go to God about the matter. Find His heart before you talk to people. You will find that He is more concerned for their welfare than you imagined.

Dear Jesus, too often I fail to represent You well to those around me because of backbiting and gossip. Thank You that Your forgiveness is always available. Let me turn to You when situations arise. Amen.

My spiritual preparation for today:

_____

_____

_____

PULLING DOWN STRONGHOLDS

*For though we walk in the flesh, we do not war according to
the flesh. For the weapons of our warfare are not carnal, but
mighty through God to the pulling down of strongholds.*
—2 CORINTHIANS 10:3-4

WHAT MEN CALL "salvation" is simply the first stage of God's
plan for our lives, which is to conform us in character and
power to the image of Jesus Christ. If we fail to see our relationship to God as such, we will allow too many areas within us
to remain unchanged. Pulling down strongholds is the demo-
lition and removal of our old ways of thinking so that the
actual presence of Jesus Christ can be manifested through us.

All successful deliverance must begin by first removing that
which defends the enemy. In speaking of spiritual warfare, the
apostle Paul enlists the word *stronghold* to define the spiritual
fortresses wherein Satan and his legions hide and are protected.
These fortresses exist in the thought patterns and ideas that
govern individuals, families, churches, communities, and even
nations. Before victory can be claimed, these strongholds must
be pulled down and Satan's armor removed. Then the mighty
weapons of the Word and the Spirit can effectively plunder
Satan's house.

> *Father, I confess that there are many strongholds in
> my mind that give shelter to the enemy. Come into
> my mind and take captive every one of my thoughts
> and make them obedient to Christ. Amen.*

MY SPIRITUAL PREPARATION FOR TODAY:

_____

_____

Day 28

The Banner of His Redemptive Mission

*As You have sent Me into the world, so
I sent them into the world.*
—John 17:18

As His followers, we are called to carry the banner of His redemptive mission. We are called to die that others may live. Therefore we must realize that before our perception develops, our love must mature until our normal attitude is one of forgiveness. Should God call us to release men from spiritual bondage, we cannot react to the confrontational things they may say. As our perception becomes more like Christ Himself and the secrets of men's hearts are revealed, we cannot even react to what men think.

We will presume we have discernment when, in truth, we are seeing through the veil of a critical spirit. We must know our weaknesses, for if we are blind to our sins, what we assume we discern in men will merely be the reflection of ourselves. Indeed, if we do not move in love, we will actually become a menace to the body of Christ.

> *O Lord, I so often fail to love without even realizing it. Help me today to get past myself long enough to see the world around me through Your eyes of love and compassion. Amen.*

My spiritual preparation for today:

_____

_____

_____

_____

An Understanding of Strongholds

The LORD is my pillar, and my fortress, and my deliverer; my God, my rock, in whom I take refuge; my shield, and the horn of my salvation, my high tower.
—PSALM 18:2

IN THE OLD Testament a stronghold was a fortified dwelling used as a means of protection from an enemy. David hid from King Saul in wilderness strongholds at Horesh. (See 1 Samuel 23:14, 19.) These were physical structures, usually caves high on a mountainside, and were very difficult to assault. It was with this imagery in mind that the inspired writers of the Bible adapted the word *stronghold* to define powerful, vigorously protected spiritual realities.

A stronghold can be a source of protection for us from the devil, as is the case when the Lord becomes our stronghold, fortress, and high tower. Or conversely, a stronghold can be a source of defense for the devil, where demonic or sinful activity is actually defended within us by our sympathetic thoughts toward evil.

> *Lord, be my fortress and stronghold of safety from the enemy. I run to You and rest in Your protection. I do not need to fear the attacks of the evil one for You are my high tower. Amen!*

MY SPIRITUAL PREPARATION FOR TODAY:

_____

_____

_____

_____

DAY 30

CRUCIFY THE REBELLIOUS NATURE

Casting down imaginations and every high thing that exalts itself against the knowledge of God, bringing every thought into captivity to the obedience of Christ.
—2 CORINTHIANS 10:5

THE APOSTLE PAUL defines a stronghold as a "high thing that exalts itself against the knowledge of God" (2 Cor. 10:5). A demonic stronghold is any type of thinking that exalts itself above the knowledge of God, thereby giving the devil a secure place of influence in an individual's thought life.

In most cases we are not talking about demonic possession. If one has given his life to Christ, he has become the property of the Son of God and is, in truth, purchased by Christ. However, Christians can be *oppressed* by demons, which can occupy unregenerated thought systems, especially if those thoughts are defended by self-deception or false doctrines. The thought "I cannot have a demon because I am a Christian" is simply untrue. A demon cannot have you in an eternal, possessive sense, but you can have a demon if you refuse to repent of your sympathetic thoughts toward evil. Your rebellion toward God provides a place for the devil in your life.

> *Jesus, I know that without You it is impossible to crucify my rebellious nature. Help me, Lord! If there be any sinful activity within me or any sympathetic thoughts toward evil, come and pull them out by the roots and fill the place they occupied with Your Holy Spirit. Amen.*

MY SPIRITUAL PREPARATION FOR TODAY:

GAINING GOD'S PERSPECTIVE

*If you will receive my words, and hide my commandments
within you, so that you incline your ear to wisdom,
and apply your heart to understanding; yes, if you
cry out for knowledge, and lift up your voice for
understanding, if you seek her as silver, and search for
her as for hidden treasures, then you will understand
the fear of the LORD, and find the knowledge of God.*
—PROVERBS 2:1–5

THERE IS A difference between having *knowledge about God*
and gaining *God's own knowledge* concerning a situation.
We need the Lord's perspective about every matter. Have we not
often made a situation worse by approaching it without truly
knowing the Lord's heart? When we see as He sees, we are positioned in a more understanding view than our own. Although
we may have problems with the people, we must remember that
Christ died for them. Certainly He loves them as much as He
loves us.

> *Dear Lord, help me to have more than knowledge
> about You; I want to have Your knowledge and
> wisdom regarding every situation in my life. Please
> give me Your heart and wisdom about the issues I'm
> facing today. Thank You! In Jesus's name I pray, amen.*

MY SPIRITUAL PREPARATION FOR TODAY:

_____

_____

_____

_____

Day 32

Walking in Great Victory

The ruler of this world is coming. He has no power over Me.
—John 14:30

You see, Satan feeds upon sin. Wherever there is a habit of sin in a believer's life, expect to find demonic activity in that area. The sin habit often becomes the dwelling place for a spirit that is robbing a believer of power and joy, and that habitation (or habit) is a stronghold.

There were no strongholds, no wrong attitudes, no faulty thinking processes in Christ's mind. Just before Jesus went to His death, He remarked that Satan had nothing in Him. We also want to be able to say that Satan has no secret area inside us, no temptation he can stage that will open the door of our soul toward evil. When the strongholds of our minds are toppled, though we may still occasionally fall into sin, we will walk in great victory.

> *Precious Jesus, close every door of temptation, uproot every wrong attitude, correct every faulty thought process, and tear down every stronghold of evil. Come quickly please, Lord! I want to walk out of darkness into Your marvelous light. Deliver me from evil today! Amen.*

My spiritual preparation for today:

_____

_____

_____

_____

_____

Changing the Spiritual Atmosphere of Your Home

Fathers, do not provoke your children to anger, but bring them up in the discipline and instruction of the Lord....Pray in the Spirit always with all kinds of prayer and supplication.
—Ephesians 6:4, 18

PERHAPS THE WORST place for gossip and faultfinding to occur is in the home. Often the prevailing spiritual atmosphere is not one of peace but is actual witchcraft coming against a child through an angry or embittered parent.

When God gave you children, He also provided love so you could pray effectively for them. Let your love express itself before God in intercessory prayer. Never spend more time complaining about your child than you do praying for him or her. If you have to keep praying for years, then do it. If the spiritual atmosphere in your home is one of "death," you are simply destroying your own life.

If you, as parents, react *without* prayer, the relationship with your child will be all the more given to the enemy! But if you respond *with* prayer, with God's help the peace can be restored in your home and the devil expelled.

> *Dear Father, being a parent is not easy; I need You. Help me to guard the spiritual atmosphere in our home, keeping it as one of peace. Thank You for Your power and help. In Jesus's name I ask this. Amen.*

My spiritual preparation for today:

_____

_____

_____

REPENTANCE PRECEDES DELIVERANCE

Create in me a clean heart, O God,
and renew a right spirit within me.
—PSALM 51:10

IF YOU HAVE been a Christian for any length of time, you have already had many strongholds broken in your life. These were broken when you repented and came to Jesus. Deliverance is often just that simple when a soul is willing. Yet, without some measure of repentance, deliverance is almost always impossible, for although a spirit may be commanded to leave, if the structure of the individual's thoughts has not been changed, his wrong attitude toward sin will welcome that spirit back.

One aspect of Christ's ministry is that "thoughts of many hearts may be revealed" (Luke 2:35). If you are truly walking with Jesus, many areas of your thinking processes will be exposed. Yet there will be a power from God to enable you to repent and receive His virtue into your life. You will see strongholds fall and victory come.

> *Heavenly Father, there are areas in my life that I have not fully surrendered to my Lord Jesus Christ. Forgive me of compromise. Give me courage to approach the pulling down of strongholds without reluctance or willful deception. In Jesus's name, amen.*

MY SPIRITUAL PREPARATION FOR TODAY:

_____

_____

_____

_____

MORE THAN CONQUERORS

In all these things we are more than
conquerors through Him who loved us.
—ROMANS 8:37

FOR ALL I have spoken concerning principalities and powers, witchcraft and curses, the most threatening battle we face today is not in the spiritual realm, nor is it on our streets or in our courts. Our greatest battle is in our hearts: the fight of faith.

God is calling us to become "more than conquerors" (Rom. 8:37). For those who overcome, there will certainly be a time when every good word God has ever promised comes to pass. We will know and experience God on the highest level.

Until then, the Lord's objective is to perfect faith in those whom He intends to use. However, true faith takes courage, for until the Word comes to pass in our lives, it will test us, and the test must, of necessity, take time; character is proven slowly. The heart that continues to trust God through the tests demonstrates that the believer genuinely knows the true nature of God and that what God has promised He is also able to perform (Rom. 4:21).

O Lord, I know that through You I am more than
a conqueror, but sometimes I do not live like that.
Today help me to stand firm in the faith, knowing
that what You have promised me will come to pass.
In Jesus's name, amen.

MY SPIRITUAL PREPARATION FOR TODAY:

_____

_____

_____

A HOUSE MADE OF THOUGHTS

*When an unclean spirit goes out of a man, it passes
through dry places seeking rest, but finds none. Then it
says, "I will return to my house from which I came." And
when it comes, it finds it empty, swept, and put in order.*
—MATTHEW 12:43–44

THE DIMENSION OF the human soul that is most similar in
disposition to the demonic realm is our carnal nature. It is
uniquely in our uncrucified thoughts and unsanctified attitudes
that unclean spirits, masking themselves as our thoughts and
hiding themselves in our attitudes, find access into our lives.

It is important to recognize that when we speak of strongholds, we are not talking about random thoughts or occasional
sins. Rather, the strongholds that affect us most are those that
are so hidden in our thinking patterns that we do not recognize
them or identify them as evil. Remember, in Matthew 12:43 Jesus
revealed that unclean spirits are seeking "rest." The sense of rest
they seek originates from being in harmony with their environment. In other words, when someone's thought life is in agreement with unbelief, fear, or habitual sin, the enemy has rest.

*Father, clean out my thought life today. Receive my
repentance now, Lord, that I might draw near to
You and see the beauty of Your holiness. In Jesus's
name I pray, amen.*

MY SPIRITUAL PREPARATION FOR TODAY:

_____

_____

_____

Delivered Souls

*Then [the unclean spirit] goes and brings with itself seven
other spirits more evil than itself, and they enter and dwell
there. And the last state of that man is worse than the first.*
—Matthew 12:45

For deliverance to bear fruit, the nature of Christ must be
assimilated into the delivered soul. Otherwise there is the
danger that the "last state of that man" might become "worse
than the first" (Matt. 12:45; 2 Pet. 2:20). Our quest is to seek to
establish the righteousness of Christ in the very area of our hearts
where Satan once dwelt. Except in cases of physical affliction or
mental torment, we should not attempt deliverance for anyone
unwilling to repent and submit their thought life to Jesus Christ.

It is significant that the process of deliverance quite often
involves a season of inner conflict and turmoil. This is a good
sign, signifying the individual's will desires to be free. We
should expect a time where we must exercise our authority in
Christ as we "resist" the devil (1 Pet. 5:8–9). Paul speaks of the
struggle of the church against principalities and powers (Eph.
6:12). There will be a period of fighting involved in the process of
pulling down strongholds, for you are breaking your agreement
with a foe who will fight to remain in your life.

*O Lord, come and overtake my thought life today so
that I might be part of that spotless bride, eagerly
awaiting You with clean thoughts, clean hands, and
a clean heart. Amen.*

My spiritual preparation for today:

_____

_____

DAY 38

THE KEYS TO UNLOCK HELL'S GATES

I am He who lives, though I was dead. Look! I am alive for-evermore. Amen. And I have the keys of Hades and of Death.
—**REVELATION 1:18**

WHEN JESUS CAME, He plainly demonstrated that He had spiritual keys that unlocked hell's gates. In fact, in His first public teaching He declared that this confrontation with hell was His main mission.

Before we dash off "binding and loosing" every evil thing we can imagine, we should remember that Jesus said of Himself, "I have the keys of Hades and of Death" (Rev. 1:18).

If we will be successful in spiritual warfare, we must go beyond trying to apply spiritual principles against the devil; we need the anointing of Jesus to set captives free, which only comes from the heart of Jesus.

In every spiritual confrontation we must first recognize that Jesus alone is God's antidote for all our world's ills. Jesus has the particular keys that can unlock the gates of hell and release captives.

Heavenly Father, let my life be an example of Your love so that the power of Christ's anointing unlocks the hellish chains of those around me and sets them free. Amen.

MY SPIRITUAL PREPARATION FOR TODAY:

_____

_____

_____

_____

REMOVING SATAN'S ARMOR

*When a strong man, fully armed, guards his own palace,
his goods are peacefully kept. But when a stronger man
than he attacks and overpowers him, he seizes all the
armor in which the man trusted and divides his spoils.*
—LUKE 11:21–22

OUR BORN-AGAIN EXPERIENCES may be widely varied on a natural level, but in the spirit realm, a very similar war was waged and won for each of us. If we could have seen into the invisible world, we would have observed the Holy Spirit working with the angels of God to destroy the enemy's first line of defense, his "armor." What exactly was this armor that protected the devil and kept us from salvation? It was our thoughts, attitudes, and opinions that were in agreement with evil.

It is foolish to assume that our salvation experience eliminated all the wrong ideas and attitudes—the strongholds—that still influence our perceptions and behavior. Yes, old things passed away, but until we are walking in the fullness of Christ, we should not assume that the process of change is over.

Mighty Jesus, Lord of the heavenly hosts, place the sword of the Spirit in my hand, the breastplate of righteousness over my heart, the belt of truth around my body, the shoes of peace on my feet, and the helmet of salvation on my mind that I might stand firm against the one who must always submit to You. All honor and glory is Yours. Amen.

MY SPIRITUAL PREPARATION FOR TODAY:

FIX YOUR EYES UPON JESUS

So we may no longer be children, tossed here and there by waves and carried about with every wind of doctrine by the trickery of men, by craftiness with deceitful scheming. But, speaking the truth in love, we may grow up in all things into Him.
—EPHESIANS 4:14–15

THE MOMENT WE accept a biblical worldview, our powers of discernment start to become active. For the most part, however, our spiritual faculties are still immature and undeveloped. Like a newborn, we see and hear, but it is difficult to bring things into focus. While we may have better clarity concerning good and evil, we usually do not know how to process what we see. We often find ourselves judging people rather than actually having revelatory insight into how to help them.

Yet the gifts of God are, in truth, living realities. As such, we should expect our powers of discernment to grow—and nothing accelerates that growth process like focusing our vision on conformity to Christ. The closer we come to abiding in Christ and His words, the more truly we can expect to understand how He thinks and what motivates His heart.

Dear Jesus, show me how to leave childish things behind. Grow me up in You today. Give me clear focus, give me vision, give me wisdom to know how to throw off those things that hinder me in pursuit of You. Amen.

MY SPIRITUAL PREPARATION FOR TODAY:

_____

_____

_____

CONFESSING YOUR NEED

As [a man] thinks in his heart, so is he.
—PROVERBS 23:7

RARE IS THE Christian who is not limited by at least one of the following strongholds: unbelief, cold love, fear, pride, unforgiveness, lust, greed, or any combination of these, as well as the possibility of many others.

Because we excuse ourselves so readily, it is difficult to discern the areas of oppression in our lives. After all, these are *our* thoughts, attitudes, and perceptions; we justify and defend our thoughts with the same degree of intensity with which we justify and defend ourselves. If we review Proverbs 23:7, we realize that the essence of who we are exists in our thought life.

Therefore, before any deliverance can truly be accomplished, we must honestly recognize and confess our need. We must stop pretending everything is all right. We must humble ourselves and seek help. Indeed, as previously mentioned, the first stronghold that God must remove is pride. For until one is willing to admit that he needs deliverance, he will never be free from strongholds.

Lord Jesus, I submit to You. I renounce my flawed, sinful, old nature, and by the grace of God and the power of Your Spirit I pull down the stronghold of unbelief that exists in my mind. Transform me into Your image as I walk with You in Your grace. Amen.

MY SPIRITUAL PREPARATION FOR TODAY:

_____

_____

_____

DAY 42

THE MYSTERY OF MAN'S IDENTITY

*What is man that You are mindful of him, or
the son of man that You care for him?*
—HEBREWS 2:6

FROM THE FATHER'S view *the mystery of man's identity
is unveiled in the life of Jesus Christ.* Christ is the "first-born among many brothers" (Rom. 8:29). He is first born of a heavenly genesis; He is the Father's plan for mankind. When we consider the mystery of humanity, we find our answer in beholding Jesus Christ. He is not only our Savior, but He is also the indwelling One who conforms us to Himself (Rom. 8:28–29; Heb. 2:10).

Let us also realize that only Jesus can be Jesus. As we yield to Him in increasing degrees of surrender, as we abide in Him and His Word abides in us, He brings forth life that is not simply like His own, but is His very life! Christ Himself living within us fulfills God's eternal purpose, which is to make man in His image. It is the presence of the Lord Jesus coming forth in us that makes the weapons of our warfare mighty, empowering our words with authority as we pull down strongholds.

> *Dear Father, forgive me, but I don't always look to Your Son as the source of my identity. I surrender to You today. Let me abide in Your presence and see my life conform to Your purpose. Amen.*

MY SPIRITUAL PREPARATION FOR TODAY:

_____

_____

_____

DEFEAT THE STRONGHOLD OF FAILURE

*But thanks be to God, who gives us the victory through
our Lord Jesus Christ! Therefore, my beloved brothers, be
steadfast, immovable, always abounding in the work of the
Lord, knowing that your labor in the Lord is not in vain.*
—1 CORINTHIANS 15:57–58

To DEAL WITH the stronghold of failure, we must make
repentance our way of life. Bear in mind also that *repentance* means "change," not merely remorse. Our thinking must
change. There are herds of erroneous thoughts roaming across
our minds, grazing upon the ever-available hay and stubble of
unbelief and failure.

Thoughts like "I will always be a failure" or "I am just a
sinner" or "I tried walking in the Spirit but it didn't work" converge and form the walls, floor, and ceiling—the building material of the stronghold of failure. To secure victory, you must
capture these wrong thoughts.

> *Jesus, I take every thought captive and bring them
> into obedience to You and Your Word. Let me find
> security in who You say I am and not what the
> world has called me or my own thoughts have condemned me to be. Because of You I am victorious. I
> will not fail. In Jesus's name, amen.*

MY SPIRITUAL PREPARATION FOR TODAY:

_____

_____

_____

_____

DAY 44

THE UPWARD CALL

*The Spirit Himself bears witness with our spirits
that we are children of God, and if children, then
heirs: heirs of God and joint-heirs with Christ.*
—ROMANS 8:16–17

IT IS SAD, but many Christians muddy along, hoping for
nothing loftier than a short reprieve from sin, guilt, and self-
condemnation. Should the lowliness of our sinful state have
veto power over the enormity of God's promises? May it never
be! For Scripture assures us that our call, even as lowly as we
feel sometimes, is an upward climb that relies upon faith in
God's abilities and our Lord's redemption. We aren't harnessed
to our flaws and weaknesses; in spirit-to-Spirit fusion we are
united to the resurrection power of Heaven! Our call is not
merely to attend church but to walk with God, whose eternal
goal has predestined us to be "conformed to the image of His
Son" (Rom. 8:29).

> *Loving heavenly Father, I am in need of Your grace
> today. I am in need of the mind of Christ. I need the
> resurrection power of Heaven to bring Your spiri-
> tual breakthrough in my life. I need a fresh infusion
> of faith to fuel the upward climb I face today. Help
> me as I press in to You, the One who provides for all
> my needs. Be the lifter of my head today. In Jesus's
> name I pray, amen.*

MY SPIRITUAL PREPARATION FOR TODAY:

_____

_____

_____

The Greatest Source of Strongholds

*When I was a child, I spoke as a child, I understood
as a child, and I thought as a child. But when I
became a man, I put away childish things.*
—1 Corinthians 13:11

PERHAPS THE GREATEST source of strongholds found in our hearts comes from the steady stream of information and experiences that continually shaped our childhood perceptions. The amount of love (or lack of love) in our home, our cultural environment, peer values and pressures, as well as fears of rejection and exposure—even our physical appearance and intelligence—all combine to form our sense of identity and our view of life.

As Christians, only the truth of Jesus Christ qualifies us to enter eternal life. He must be our primary mentor and ultimate instructor; otherwise we will simply conform to the limitations and patterns of our worldly teachers, and we will never rise higher than the standards of our culture. Our teachers and fathers more than likely did the best they could. Yet our goal is not simply to do the deeds of our fathers but to do the deeds of Jesus.

> *Dear Jesus, I am ready to grow up in You, to leave behind those childhood perceptions that shaped my thinking and my nature. Reshape me so that I might conform once again to God's original design and purpose for my life—to be in relationship with Him as He partners with me to advance His kingdom. Amen.*

My spiritual preparation for today:

_____

_____

THE VOICE OF LOVE

Beloved, if God so loved us, we must also love one another.
—1 JOHN 4:11

I KNOW THAT, FOR some, to love as Christ has loved us remains an ideal too far to reach. Therefore let us start small and bring this task close to home. Rather than attempting to love everyone, let us reduce our challenge and determine to love just one person. Now I do not mean stop loving family or those you already love. I mean add just one person and love that individual in a greater way.

This person may be a lost neighbor or a backslidden friend; he or she might be a sick acquaintance or an elderly person from church or a child in pain. The Lord will lead you and help you reach your goal of genuinely loving just one soul.

Come to this experiment without seeking to correct him or her, unless they themselves ask for advice. Pray daily for the individual. And as you listen to the voice of God's love, something inside you will flower and open naturally toward higher realms of discernment. Inspired by God, impulses and ideas born of love will increase in your relationship with others, and the knowledge and insights you gain from loving just one will become a natural part of your personality in loving many. Discernment will grow as you love just one.

> *Dear Lord, take my hand today and help me to understand what it means to love just one person as You love them. Thank You, Jesus. Amen.*

MY SPIRITUAL PREPARATION FOR TODAY:

_____

_____

NEW IN CHRIST

Therefore, if any man is in Christ, he is a new creature. Old things have passed away. Look, all things have become new.
—2 CORINTHIANS 5:17

WHEN YOU WERE born again, you received the very Spirit of God, and through His Spirit you were birthed into another realm: the kingdom of Heaven. Though your feet are still on earth, through the vehicle of the Holy Spirit you are united to the actual person of Jesus Christ, who is seated at the throne of God. Even as your limbs are attached to your torso, so your heart is attached to the power of God. You are never alone. Christ is always with you. What you were as a person prior to salvation, you will never be again!

Everything, even your intelligence and physical appearance, is now subject to change for the better. This is why our culture and the boundaries of worldly knowledge must not be allowed to rule over us, for old limitations are destined to go. New faith and hope should be growing within you daily.

How do we attain such a wonderful new beginning? We receive the Spirit of Christ into our hearts to empower us. We study the words of Christ to direct us. And whatever we find in us that is not like Jesus, we crucify.

> *O Father! Don't leave me as I am, please! Let new faith and new hope rise up and obliterate anything of the old nature that wants to rule my heart. Take me to that place of new beginnings with You. Amen.*

MY SPIRITUAL PREPARATION FOR TODAY:

_____

_____

THE SHELTER OF GRACE

So that just as sin reigned in death, grace might reign through righteousness unto eternal life through Jesus Christ our Lord.
—ROMANS 5:21

IT IS ONLY our exaggerated sense of self-righteousness that prevents us from looking honestly at ourselves. As Christians, we know the Holy Spirit dwells within us, but we must also become aware of where we are tolerating sin if we will be successful in our war against the devil.

Therefore be specific when you submit yourself to God. Do not rationalize your sins and failures. The sacrifice of Jesus Christ is a perfect shelter of grace enabling all men to look honestly at their needs. Accordingly, be honest with God. He will not be horrified or shocked by your sins. God loved you without restraint even when sin was rampant within you; how much more will He continue to love you as you seek His grace to be free from iniquity?

> *Father God, forgive me for failing to acknowledge my sin and confess it to You. Show me any unconfessed wrongdoing that I might repent and find Your grace and love waiting to forgive me. Amen.*

MY SPIRITUAL PREPARATION FOR TODAY:

_____

_____

_____

_____

_____

TRUE FASTING

*Blessed are those who hunger and thirst for
righteousness, for they shall be filled.*
—MATTHEW 5:6

A T ITS ESSENCE, the purpose of a fast is to help us reach our spiritual destination faster, hence the name *fast*. The goal of our hunger is for righteousness to prevail, either in us personally or in our family, church, city, or nation. Fasting takes us there faster.

Yet we must not allow our fast to become a form of self-inflicted punishment. Fasting is not about "neglecting of the body" (Col. 2:20–23). In truth, a fast is a gift of grace—an opportunity to engage the Lord in an extended time of desire. During the time you would have nourished your body, nourish yourself spiritually instead. Draw closer to the Lord. Read the Word of God, memorize Scriptures, or pray for yourself and others.

Isaiah 58:6–7 tells us that a fast can also be a time to show God's love to others. Therefore, when you are fasting from food, consider also ways to help the disadvantaged and hurting. You might even devote your food money to a relief agency who gives care to suffering people in destitute places.

> *Lord, help me to choose the type of fast that You have chosen, to loosen the bonds of wickedness and to let the oppressed go free. Let me share my food with the hungry and bring the homeless and poor into my house. In Your name, amen.*

MY SPIRITUAL PREPARATION FOR TODAY:

_____

_____

DAY 50

THE STRONGHOLD OF OUR EXPERIENCES

Jesus Christ is the same yesterday, and today, and forever.
—HEBREWS 13:8

EVERYONE WHO HAS a promise from God will pass through situations that seem to be the exact opposite of what they expected. We may value our experiences, but what must rule our hearts is the Word of God. In other words, even though we were not healed, we should not conclude that healing is not for today. God's provision is eternal, which means that until Heaven and earth pass away, He has provided for all our needs. In regard to sin, though we might repeatedly stumble, we must continue to believe God for grace to overcome. We must give ourselves room to grow into new insights. We must never surrender our faith in God's Word! If the conclusions we draw from our experiences leave us thinking that Jesus is not the same today as He was in the Gospels, the conclusion we have drawn is wrong. It is a stronghold that must be pulled down.

> *Father, let my faith triumph over the experiences of my life until all of my experiences come into conformity with Your living Word. Guide me to that place of no surrender, where Jesus is the same yesterday, today, and forever! Amen!*

MY SPIRITUAL PREPARATION FOR TODAY:

_____

_____

_____

_____

_____

A FAST FROM JUDGING

*Take away the yoke from your midst, the pointing
of the finger, and speaking wickedness.*
—ISAIAH 58:9

SELF-RIGHTEOUS JUDGING, FAULTFINDING, loveless criticisms, and slander are all things that many Christians do without conscience or regret. If, however, we remove these things from our lives and give ourselves to a walk of love, the result is profound.

I want to introduce a new concept: *the fast from judging.* When I have mentioned this type of fast to others, it is interesting to watch their reactions. "What will we think about?" they query. I am not saying we should fast from thinking. No, I am saying only this: After we have thought about some issue of life, fast from letting our concluding thoughts be those of judgment. Rather, let our thoughts end in prayer for mercy, redemption, and forgiveness.

You see, the instinct to judge and criticize is a curse upon the church, and it brings death upon us as individuals. A curse? Death? Yes, every time we judge we are simultaneously judged by God, and each time we condemn another, we ourselves are condemned (Matt. 7:1–2; Luke 6:37).

> *Father, I commit to fast from judging today. Put a check in my spirit, please, each time I begin to drift away from Your walk of love, and guide me back to the only path that leads to life, to Jesus! Thank You, Father. Amen.*

MY SPIRITUAL PREPARATION FOR TODAY:

_____

_____

DAY 52

CAPTURE YOUR THOUGHTS
OF CONDEMNATION

Be transformed by the renewing of your mind.
—ROMANS 12:2

CAPTURE THE THOUGHT "I am a failure!" Repent of it, asking the Lord to forgive you of your unbelief. Let your mind be renewed by the Word of God, which states, "I can do all things because of Christ who strengthens me" (Phil. 4:13). Even though you have failed and will fail again in the future, now because Christ is in your life, you can confidently proclaim, "Though I was a failure, my sufficiency comes from God, not myself. He causes all things to work for my good so that nothing is impossible if I keep faith in Him."

By capturing your self-condemning thoughts and identifying yourself as God's child, you are tearing down a stronghold of defeat that once oppressed you. In its place you are building a godly stronghold of faith, which is built upon the Word of God. With the old stronghold exposed and the thought patterns of defeatism coming down, the Word of God will begin to renew you in the spirit of your mind. You will need to persevere in your victory, but as you do, you will begin to walk in tremendous power and peace. You will enter the godly stronghold of faith.

Dear God, forgive me for believing lying, self-condemning thoughts that defeat me and keep me from accomplishing Your purpose. Today I will press into Your presence until there is room for nothing else. Amen.

MY SPIRITUAL PREPARATION FOR TODAY:

_____

_____

THE STRONGHOLD OF WRONG DOCTRINES

Now the Spirit clearly says that in the last times
some will depart from the faith and pay attention
to seducing spirits and doctrines of devils.
—1 TIMOTHY 4:1

STRONGHOLDS IN OUR life can come from false church doctrines and teachings. Jesus warned, "Take heed that no one deceives you" (Matt. 24:4). We can be led by another person, but we must take responsibility that we are not *misled* by that individual. We must study and know the Bible ourselves. If we do not, how can we discern if there is error in the teachings we hear? No teacher is so true, no ministry so pure that we can blindly let them lead us. They may lead us, but our eyes must be open and our ears sensitive to the confirming voice of the Holy Spirit. Even true teachers can innocently communicate false doctrines. It does not matter how sincere our Bible teachers are. If what they are teaching does not lead us into greater surrender to Christ's love, holiness, and power, their theology can actually limit us and oppress our spiritual growth.

The safest way to insure that no one misleads us is to see to it we do not mislead ourselves. We must stay honest with God and sensitive to His love and His Word.

> *Father God, make my eyes always open and my ears*
> *always sensitive to the confirming voice of Your Holy*
> *Spirit. Teach me Your Word that I might build my*
> *life upon its truth and nothing else. Amen.*

MY SPIRITUAL PREPARATION FOR TODAY:

FRESH MERCY

Blessed are the merciful, for they shall obtain mercy.
—MATTHEW 5:7

JUDGING PEOPLE IS not discernment. When we see something wrong, instead of only turning critical, we must learn to pray for mercy for that situation. We may still see what is wrong, but now we are harnessing our energies and seeking to redeem what is wrong by the power of Christ's love.

When we resist the impulse to judge or condemn and instead pray for mercy, an amazing thing happens: *fresh mercy opens before us.* You see, in every moment of every day there are two paths in front of us: one leads to increased mercy in our lives while the other leads to a life of obstacles and difficulties. How do we receive more mercy? The key to a life blessed by God's mercy is to give mercy to those around us (Matt. 18:21–35).

> *Heavenly Father, make me mindful today that Your mercies are new every morning, for me and for everyone. Help me to remember Your great mercy toward me when I am tempted to withhold mercy from others. Should any critical, judgmental spirit try and rise up within me today, snuff it out quickly so that my heart might gravitate toward Your heart of mercy. Great is Your faithfulness, O Lord!*

MY SPIRITUAL PREPARATION FOR TODAY:

_____

_____

_____

_____

OUR CONTINUAL TRANSFORMATION

But we all, seeing the glory of the Lord with unveiled faces, as in a mirror, are being transformed into the same image from glory to glory by the Spirit of the Lord.
—2 CORINTHIANS 3:18

LET IT BE established in your attitudes that the goal and purpose of your salvation is that you be conformed to the likeness of Christ. Is it not written, "Whom He foreknew, He predestined to be conformed to the image of His Son" (Rom. 8:29)? The same Lord who conquered the devil and liberated your heart in salvation is working still to renew your mind.

As long as we recognize that our salvation is a continual transformation, and that we are changing from "glory to glory" (2 Cor. 3:18) into the image of Christ, we should not be discouraged by the strongholds we discover, nor will occasional or momentary setbacks render us impotent. As we see our need, we rejoice in knowing it is only a matter of time before another obstacle is removed!

Father, continue to transform my heart and let me be changed from glory to glory. Remove the obstacles in my life and draw me even closer to You! Yes, and amen!

MY SPIRITUAL PREPARATION FOR TODAY:

_____

_____

_____

_____

_____

God's Highest Purpose

*So that you may declare the goodness of Him who has
called you out of darkness into His marvelous light.*
—1 Peter 2:9

Most Christians only engage in spiritual warfare with a hope of either relieving present distresses or attaining a "normal" existence. However, the purpose of all aspects of spirituality, warfare included, is to bring us into the image of Christ. Nothing, not worship or warfare, neither love nor deliverance, is truly attainable if we miss the singular objective of our faith: Christlikeness.

While we may not want to hear this, many of our spiritual conflicts simply are not going to cease until the character of the Lord Jesus is formed in our hearts. The Father's goal in deliverance is much more than simply seeing our burdens or the devil taken off our backs. Indeed, the specific purpose toward which God steers the working of all things in our lives is our conformity "to the image of His Son"; the Father's purpose in our salvation was that Jesus would become "the firstborn among many brothers" (Rom. 8:29). In other words, the way to realize God's ultimate victory is to reach toward His ultimate goal, which is complete transformation into the likeness of Christ.

*Take me today, Father, and form the character of Jesus
in my heart. Don't leave me the way I am, please! I
need Your breakthrough in my life today. Amen.*

My spiritual preparation for today:

_____

_____

_____

Mercy Triumphs Over Judgment

*For he who has shown no mercy will have judgment
without mercy, for mercy triumphs over judgment.*
—James 2:13

THERE ARE CHRISTIANS I know who have not made spiritual progress for years. They attend church and they tithe, yet they maintain a self-righteous, judgmental attitude. They always have something negative to say about others. As such, they position themselves under God's judgment. Their capacity to receive divine mercy is closed because they do not show mercy toward others.

Are you pondering why your version of Christianity doesn't quite feel like the abundant life Jesus promised in John 10:10? Perhaps it is because you are too judgmental. It is a natural tendency in most people. Indeed, recall how even the Lord's disciples wanted to call fire down upon the Samaritans. Yet Jesus rebuked His disciples, saying that they did not know what spirit they were of (Luke 9:51–56). Let us, therefore, discern "what spirit" we are of. Let us remember that mercy triumphs over judgment; if we strive to be merciful, God promises He will respond to us as we have responded to others.

> *O God, teach me to say no to ungodly thoughts and
> behaviors. I want to live a self-controlled and godly
> life today and every day. Amen.*

My spiritual preparation for today:

_____

_____

_____

ZERO TOLERANCE FOR THE ENEMY

*If your whole body, then, is full of light, no part
being dark, the whole body will be full of light, as
when the shining candle gives you light.*
—LUKE 11:36

WE MUST REALIZE that it is not Satan who defeats us; it is
our openness to him. To perfectly subdue the devil we
must walk in the "shelter of the Most High" (Ps. 91:1). Satan is
tolerated for one purpose: the warfare between the devil and
God's saints thrusts us into Christlikeness, where the nature of
Christ becomes our only place of rest and security. God allows
warfare to facilitate His eternal plan, which is to make man in
His image. (See Genesis 1:26.)

Are you troubled by demons of fear or doubt? Submit *those*
areas to God, repenting of your unbelief, and then yield yourself to Christ's faith within you. Are you troubled with spirits
of lust and shame? Present those very areas of sin to God,
repenting of your old nature, drawing upon the forgiveness of
Christ and His purity of heart.

> *O Father, I come before You now, presenting all
> areas of sin in my life. I repent of my old nature.
> Take me to that fount of every blessing where Your
> heart overflows to all. In Jesus's name I pray, amen.*

MY SPIRITUAL PREPARATION FOR TODAY:

_____

_____

_____

_____

Destroy the Stronghold of Fear

There is no fear in love, but perfect love casts out fear.
—1 John 4:18

GOD DOES NOT want us in bondage. He has not given us a "spirit of fear," but of love, power, and a sound mind (2 Tim. 1:7, kjv). Therefore it's wise to look within yourself at some of the thoughts and experiences that may have formed the structure of this tormenting fortress of fear. You may not even remember the incident(s), but since then you have refused to place yourself in situations where you can become vulnerable to criticism.

Your experience tells you that if you try something new, especially in front of people, you may be embarrassed and rejected. To counter this, a whole series of reactions emerges in your mind. You sit back when you should step forward. You are silent when you should be speaking. That silent, fearful withdrawal into yourself has become a house made of thoughts, wherein dwells a spirit of fear.

You can be delivered from that oppression on your soul by releasing and forgiving those who hurt you. The stronghold of fear will be replaced by the stronghold of love.

> *Blessed Lord, I repent for accommodating mistrust, fear, and insecurity. I release those who have wounded me in the past, and I speak to the spirit of fear—it has no place in my life. In Jesus's name, amen.*

My spiritual preparation for today:

_____

_____

_____

PUNISHMENT VS. BLESSING

*But he who does wrong will receive for the wrong
which he has done, and there is no partiality.*
—COLOSSIANS 3:25

THE DEVIL HAS no power to originate anything; he can only manipulate what already is under the judgment or wrath of God. All sin is under God's curse, and whatever is under God's curse is accessible to evil spirits.

Christians are not exempt from this. If we sow to the flesh, we will reap corruption and eventually become vulnerable to evil spirits if we fail to repent and walk humbly with our God.

God's greatest blessing abides upon the nature of Christ. Wherever we are walking as Jesus walked, in love and purity of heart, we are enriched and protected by God's blessing. Even the desire to walk like Christ draws the Father's blessing, for such a soul is quick to repent; its humility draws grace from God.

*Precious Holy Spirit, I know that true repentance
and humility are the keys to receiving grace and forgiveness for my sin. Let me walk in love and purity
so that I might receive Your blessing today. Amen.*

MY SPIRITUAL PREPARATION FOR TODAY:

_____

_____

_____

_____

_____

_____

WRONG FOCUS

Let us look to Jesus, the author and finisher of
our faith, who for the joy that was set before Him
endured the cross, despising the shame, and is
seated at the right hand of the throne of God.
—HEBREWS 12:2

THERE ARE OCCASIONS when your battle against the devil is actually a digression from the higher purpose God has for you. Intercessors and warfare leaders take note: there is a demon whose purpose is to lure one's mind into hell. If we were to name this spirit, we would call it "Wrong Focus." You may be fighting this very spirit if you are continually seeing evil spirits in people or in the material world around you. The ultimate goal of this demon is to produce mental illness in saints who move in deliverance. Listen very carefully: we are not called to focus on the battle or the devil, except when that battle hinders our immediate transformation into Christ's likeness. *Our calling is to focus on Jesus.* The work of the devil, however, is to draw our eyes from Jesus. Satan's first weapon always involves luring our eyes from Christ. Turn toward Jesus, and almost immediately the battle vanishes.

> *Jesus, I know I am guilty of paying far too much attention to what the devil is doing and far too little attention to what You are doing. Save me from myself, Lord! Oh, that I would learn the joy of keeping my eyes fixed on You. I ask this in Your precious name, amen.*

MY SPIRITUAL PREPARATION FOR TODAY:

GOD'S ANTIDOTE FOR EVIL

As the bird by flitting, as the swallow by flying, so
the curse without cause will not alight.
—PROVERBS 26:2

THE BASIS OF how most witchcraft and occult power works is this: Satan is limited to what is under God's judgment. The devil cannot revoke what God has cursed, and he cannot harm what God has blessed.

God will not allow a curse to land without cause. Sin is the landing strip in a person's soul upon which a curse alights. Just as "death" entered the world "through sin" (Rom. 5:12), so death cannot enter where there is no sin.

Thus the key to walking free from the effects of witchcraft is to walk in obedience to God and under the shelter of His blessing. It is here that we find God's antidote for evil. For Satan cannot curse what God has blessed.

> *Lord, when You have granted Satan permission to sift me, I pray that I can stand strong and let my life serve Your higher purposes. I know that nothing can touch me without Your permission. I pray that I will always walk in obedience to You and remain under the shelter of the Most High. In Jesus's name, amen.*

MY SPIRITUAL PREPARATION FOR TODAY:

_____

_____

_____

_____

_____

KEEPING A PROPER BALANCE

The Lord of Hosts is with us.
—PSALM 46:7

THE TRUE GIFT called "discernment of spirits" is a balanced gift that enables you to recognize at least as many angelic spirits as you do evil spirits. The proper manifestation of this gift has a much more positive focus than what commonly masquerades as discernment.

An example of the proper balance in discernment is seen in 2 Kings. The Syrian army had surrounded Dothan, a city in Israel, much to the consternation of the prophet Elisha's servant. To calm his attendant's fright, Elisha prayed that his servant's eyes would be opened. He then encouraged his servant, saying, "Do not be afraid, for there are more with us than with them" (2 Kings 6:16). As the Lord opened the servant's eyes, he saw what Elisha saw: "The mountain was full of horses and chariots of fire surrounding Elisha" (v. 17).

In spiritual warfare the battle is never limited to an "us against them" human affair. It always includes those "with us" against those "with them." True discernment is as fully aware of the vast multitude of angels loyal to God as it is aware of the activity of the demonic realm—and it is aware that the angelic hosts on our side are both stronger and more numerous than the enemy.

> *Jesus! Jesus! Jesus! Jesus! Open my eyes today that I might see the seemingly unconquerable battles in my life surrounded by Your angels. You are victorious! Amen!*

MY SPIRITUAL PREPARATION FOR TODAY:

_____

_____

CHRIST OUR REFUGE

He has delivered us from the power of darkness and has transferred us into the kingdom of His dear Son, in whom we have redemption through His blood, the forgiveness of sins.
—COLOSSIANS 1:13–14

IN THE PUREST sense Christ alone is the divine antidote against curses and the assault of witchcraft. The combination of Jesus's work on the cross and His nature in our hearts provides a perfect haven for all who flee to Him. In Him there is no darkness at all; if we are in Him, we are therefore sheltered from the effects of God's judgment against sin as well as from Satan's exploitation of what God has cursed.

Apart from Christ, humanity exists unprotected against witchcraft. However, Christ is not only God's plan of refuge against witchcraft; He is also a refuge against the entire realm of sin and death. The fact is, all mankind has sinned and fallen short of the glory of God. God's judgment upon mankind is not to condemn us, but to compel us to run to Christ, who alone is our shelter in this world.

> *Create in me a clean heart, O Lord, and put a right spirit within me. Let me walk in such Christlike purity that I can spot the witchcraft trying to operate against my family, my church, and me. Thank You for the protection and refuge You've provided through Jesus. In Jesus's name I pray, amen.*

MY SPIRITUAL PREPARATION FOR TODAY:

_____

_____

_____

PEACE IS THE PROOF

The God of peace will soon crush Satan under your feet.
—ROMANS 16:20

TO WAGE EFFECTIVE spiritual warfare, you must understand and use spiritual authority. Spiritual authority, however, is not forcing your will upon another person. When you have spiritual authority, you have established God's peace in an area that once was full of conflict and oppression. Therefore to truly be able to move in authority, you must first have peace.

When you maintain peace during warfare, it is a crushing deathblow to satanic oppression and fear. Your victory never comes from your emotions or your intellect. Your victory comes by refusing to judge by what your eyes see or your ears hear and by trusting that what God has promised will come to pass.

You will never know Christ's victory in its fullness until you stop reacting humanly to your circumstances. When you truly have authority over something, you can look at that thing without worry, fear, or intimidation. *Your peace is the proof of your victory.*

> *Dear Jesus, help me today to subdue every storm in my life with Your authority and perfect peace. Give me a renewed confidence in Your love. I want to stand today on the solid rock of spiritual authority that You won on the cross. Make me unshakable today, Lord. Amen.*

MY SPIRITUAL PREPARATION FOR TODAY:

_____

_____

_____

THE GIFT

*Blessed be the God and Father of our Lord Jesus
Christ, who has blessed us with every spiritual
blessing in the heavenly places in Christ.*
—EPHESIANS 1:3

IN AN ETERNAL sense, from the first moment we come to
Christ, all our sins are "legally" paid for with Christ's blood,
and all curses are broken at Christ's cross. Spiritually speaking,
we were delivered from the domain of darkness and transferred
into the kingdom of His Son (Col. 1:13).

This deliverance is true wealth laid up for us in Heaven's
bank. However, if we do not draw upon it and use it, we will
remain poor and spiritually impoverished.

Thus a twofold experience occurred when we were born
again: we received every spiritual blessing in the heavenly
places in Christ, and we embarked on a journey of faith and
obedience to appropriate them.

> *Father, I run to You, my strong tower, as my refuge
> from the realm of sin and death. May I access daily
> the true wealth of deliverance that You have laid up
> for me in the bank of Heaven. Thank You for the
> blessings You have for me as I follow You in faith
> and obedience along life's journey. Amen.*

MY SPIRITUAL PREPARATION FOR TODAY:

_____

_____

_____

_____

WALK IN PEACE, WALK IN POWER

*Do not be frightened by your adversaries. This is a sign to them
of their destruction, but of your salvation, and this from God.*
—PHILIPPIANS 1:28

PEACE IS SPIRIT power. Peace is an attribute of the Holy
Spirit, and when you are walking in peace, you are walking
in power. A peacemaker is not merely someone who protests
against war; he is one who is inwardly so yielded to Christ in
spirit and purpose that he can be called a son of God. (See Matthew 5:9.) Where he goes, God goes, and where God goes, he
goes. He is fearless, calm, and bold. Peace emanates from him
the way light and heat radiate from fire.

Satan's arsenal consists of such things as fear, worry, doubt,
and self-pity. Every one of these weapons robs us of peace and
leaves us troubled inside. Do you want to discern where the
enemy is coming against you? In the network of your relationships, wherever you do not have peace, you have war. Conversely,
wherever you have peace, you have victory. When Satan hurls
his darts against you, the more peace you have during adversity,
the more truly you are walking in Christ's victory. The very fact
that you are "not...frightened" (Phil. 1:28) by your adversary is
a sign that you have authority over him.

> *Jesus, when the fiery darts of the enemy come at me,
> I will remember Your peace in the midst of battle. I
> bring my fears, worries, doubts, and any self-pity to
> the foot of Your cross and leave them there. Amen.*

MY SPIRITUAL PREPARATION FOR TODAY:

_____

_____

GENERATIONAL PATTERNS OF SIN

*And they might not be as their fathers, a
stubborn and rebellious generation.*
—PSALM 78:8

THOUGH OUR SPIRITS are now alive to God, our souls are still imperfect. If we willfully harbor rebellion toward God, we still leave ourselves exposed to witchcraft and the effects of curses.

It is also true that we ourselves may not have sinned, but we might be living under the curse of ancestral sins. These are the sins that have been passed down to us from our parents. To break ancestral curses, we must identify the un-Christ-like behavior we have inherited from our forefathers and then renounce it. Submitting our hearts to Christ for cleansing and ongoing transformation, we determine to build our lives upon the nature of Christ.

> *Lord, help me to break any ancestral curses through Your power as I renounce any and all un-Christ-like behavior that has been passed down to me. In Jesus's name, amen.*

MY SPIRITUAL PREPARATION FOR TODAY:

_____

_____

_____

_____

_____

_____

GOD IS WITH US

*Even though I walk through the valley of the shadow
of death, I will fear no evil; for You are with me.*
—PSALM 23:4

IN THE BATTLES of life your peace is actually a weapon.
Indeed, your confidence declares that you are not falling for
the lies of the devil. You see, the first step toward having spiritual authority over the adversary is having peace in spite of our
circumstances. When Jesus confronted the devil, He did not
confront Satan with His emotions or in fear. Knowing that the
devil was a liar, He simply refused to be influenced by any other
voice than God's. His peace overwhelmed Satan. His authority
then shattered the lie, which sent demons fleeing.

Only God's peace will quell your fleshly reactions in battle.
The source of God's peace is God Himself. Indeed, "Before the
throne was a sea of glass like crystal" (Rev. 4:6). The glass sea is
a symbol: there are no ripples, no waves, no anxieties troubling
God. The Lord is never worried, never in a hurry or without an
answer. The sea around Him is perfectly still and totally calm.
All our victories flow out from being seated here with Him.

> *Dear Lord, let my victories today flow from that
> place before Your throne where there are no anxieties,
> where everything is perfectly still and totally calm in
> Your magnificent presence. I refuse to be influenced
> today by any voice other than Your voice. Amen.*

MY SPIRITUAL PREPARATION FOR TODAY:

_____

_____

_____

RIGHTEOUS JUDGMENT

*Do not judge according to appearance, but
practice righteous judgment.*
—JOHN 7:24

WHEN I URGE people to not be judgmental, I am not saying, don't discern. Spiritual discernment is an art form, while judging by outer appearance is an instinct of the flesh. I am saying we must learn how to wait, listen, and, in meekness, discern the higher way of Christ.

Yet inevitably there are still questions. What about the Lord's admonition not to judge according to appearance, "but practice righteous judgment" (John 7:24)? What is righteous judgment?

In discussing this with others, I've noticed that the words *righteous* and *judgment* seem to be all that some read in the verse. However, the first part of the verse explains, at least partially, the second half: righteous judgment is that which is "not…according to appearance." Righteous judgment comes from another source, that which is higher than the instincts of the flesh.

> *Father, help me today to stop judging by outward appearance and start practicing righteous judgment that comes from the discernment You provide. In Jesus's name, amen.*

MY SPIRITUAL PREPARATION FOR TODAY:

_____

_____

_____

_____

_____

REST BEFORE RULE

*And He raised us up and seated us together
in the heavenly places in Christ Jesus.*
—EPHESIANS 2:6

BEFORE YOU GO into warfare, recognize that it is not you that the devil is afraid of; it is Christ in you! We have been raised up and seated with Christ in heavenly places (Eph. 2:6). This is why the Holy Spirit continues to speak to us that worship of God is our first response in battle. Position yourself in the presence of God. Sit, at rest, in the knowledge that Christ has already made your enemies the footstool for your feet. From a position of rest the Word of the Lord continues, "The LORD shall send your mighty scepter out of Zion; rule in the midst of your enemies" (Ps. 110:2).

Rest precedes rule. Peace precedes power. Do not seek to rule over the devil until you are submitting to God's rule over you. The focal point of all victory comes from seeking God until you find Him, and having found Him, allowing His presence to fill your spirit with His peace. From full assurance at His right hand, as you rest in His victory, so will you rule in the midst of your enemies.

> *Dear heavenly Father, I want to rule in the midst of my enemies today. Let Christ in me send the devil running! Oh, that You would find me at Your feet now, resting in Your presence as You stretch forth Your mighty right arm on my behalf. In Jesus's name, amen.*

MY SPIRITUAL PREPARATION FOR TODAY:

_____

_____

FULL OF GRACE AND TRUTH

God is love. Whoever lives in love lives in God, and God in him.
—1 JOHN 4:16

THERE IS A difference between discerning a need that you are determined to pray for and simply finding fault, which often degrades into gossip and slander. God does not "call" a person into "a ministry of judging others" because such a one has always been fearless to "tell it as it is." Faultfinding is not a gift of the Spirit.

If your judgment is truly from God, it will not be an isolated gift. You will have humility, love, and lowliness of mind as well. *Righteous judgment proves itself genuine by the virtues that support and present it.*

All the virtues of the Spirit—love, joy, peace, gentleness, etc.—should be functionally evident in your character. If so, you will be known to be gentle, loving, lowly of mind, and wise. When you bring a righteous judgment, your character affirms that your judgment is not an emotional reaction, but you come as one sent from God—like Christ, full of grace and truth. You speak as an individual who is seriously concerned with bettering the life of others.

> *Dear Lord, I am weary of faultfinding, sickened by gossip, and exhausted by slander. Take me today into that place of Your perfect love and keep me there until I can emerge with the virtues of Your Spirit evident in my words and actions. Amen.*

MY SPIRITUAL PREPARATION FOR TODAY:

_____

_____

WILL YOU RECOGNIZE HIM?

*Now when Joshua was by Jericho, he looked up
and saw a man standing in front of him. In his
hand was His drawn sword. Joshua went to Him
and said, "Are You for us or for our enemies?"*
—JOSHUA 5:13

OF ALL THE names that the heavenly Father could have given His Son, it is most significant that He chose the name *Jesus*, for Jesus is the Greek form of *Joshua*. Joshua, you recall, was the Hebrew general who led God's people into war. To be prepared for greater victories, we need a greater revelation of Jesus Christ; we need to see Him as He will be revealed in the last moments of this age: a holy warrior, dressed for battle.

Perhaps you have been through a time where the tip of Christ's sword seemed aimed straight at your heart. Let me reassure you, God is for you. In fact, it is His expressed purpose to release this same sword of the Spirit, which is the Word of God (Eph. 6:17), through your words and prayers. But before the Lord's sword will come through your mouth, it must first pass through your heart.

> *Jesus, give me a new revelation of You today as Lord
> of the angel armies, Captain of the heavenly host. I
> need to see the impossible done through Your power
> in my life, today and every day. Amen.*

MY SPIRITUAL PREPARATION FOR TODAY:

_____

_____

_____

_____

BEING FIT FOR BATTLE

The LORD shall go forth like a mighty man; He shall stir up zeal like a man of war. He shall cry out, yes, raise a war cry; He shall prevail against His enemies.
—ISAIAH 42:13

ISAIAH TELLS US that the Lord will go forth like a warrior. We have known the Lord as our Savior and our Shepherd. These revelations of our beloved Master are no less true because a new aspect of His nature is revealed. It is simply that this new dimension is so startlingly different from how we have known Him. Be of good cheer, this frightening Warrior King, with His sword drawn, with the shout of war upon His lips, is the same blessed Savior who died on the cross for our sins.

> *Dear Jesus, come and be the Lord of my life today, not because of who I am or who I associate myself with, but because of who You are. Unveil Yourself in my life as You fit me for battle. Remove any false concepts, ideas, or images of You that are untrue and replace them with Your truth. Help me to understand that You are Lord of all, not just my narrow little world. Grow me, mature me, and make me more like You. Amen.*

MY SPIRITUAL PREPARATION FOR TODAY:

_____

_____

_____

_____

_____

FOLLOW THE LAMB!

The armies in heaven...followed Him.
—REVELATION 19:14

IN SCRIPTURE WE have a picture of the proper balance in all warfare: "The armies in heaven...followed *Him*." The armies in Heaven *follow!* Who do they follow? *Jesus!* If we will be victorious, we must follow Jesus as our Lord and King.

Therefore be very conscious and very careful to be a follower of the Lord and receive training from Him. Your attack against the strongholds of hell will be in the areas of your knowledge. Satan, on the other hand, will counterattack in the areas of your ignorance.

What you will learn by obeying the Lord on the actual battleground will far exceed that which any book will provide. Place your confidence securely in the Lord as you follow *Him*.

> *Father in Heaven, Lord of Hosts, tear down the mountains in my life. Declare Your thoughts to me. Make my darkness into light. Let my feet tread on the high places of the earth for Your name's sake. Amen.*

MY SPIRITUAL PREPARATION FOR TODAY:

_____

_____

_____

_____

_____

_____

Right Doctrines Wrongly Applied

Study to show yourself approved by God, a workman who need not be ashamed, rightly dividing the word of truth.
—2 Timothy 2:15

The story of Job is not only about an innocent man suffering unjustly from a satanic attack; the bulk of the story concerns the suffering Job endured from his three friends—Eliphaz, Bildad, and Zophar (and later Elihu). These men, religious scholars of their day, were friends of Job who during his distress became his accusers.

In defense of Job's friends, they began speaking with reverence, weeping, and compassion (a place we might consider taking before we offer our opinions). However, it is plain that their religious opinions outweighed their sympathies toward Job.

Additionally it must be noted that the basis of their accusations rested upon generally true biblical principles. The problem was not with their doctrines but with their application. If Job was a sinner, most of what they had said would be applicable, but he wasn't a sinner. He was the most righteous man on earth. Job's friends had right doctrines that were wrongly applied, and in their religious pride they did not have enough humility to see they could be wrong.

> *O Lord, I confess that I am guilty of religious pride that has caused me to mishandle Your Word of truth. Forgive my lack of humility. It has been an open door to the enemy. Come into my heart now and purge it of pride and arrogance. In Jesus's name, amen.*

My spiritual preparation for today:

_____

_____

THE WARRIOR KING

The LORD shall go forth like a mighty man...He shall...raise a war cry; He shall prevail against His enemies.
—ISAIAH 42:13

WITHIN THE RANKS of the advancing church Jesus is raising a war cry. Can you hear His shout in the intercession? There is new authority being raised up, a new generation whose voice thunders with the cry of prophetic prayer. Through the church Christ Himself is prevailing against His enemies. Indeed, the gates of hell shall not stand against the church Jesus is building (Matt. 16:18). The hour has come for us to grow in all aspects into Him who is our head, even Christ, the Warrior King!

> *Dear Jesus, High King of Heaven! Let me be an agent of change in the church for unity in the body. In the power of Your Spirit help us, Your bride, to cast off false illusions and strife and all jealousies that come from the pit of hell. Show us how to stand victorious, with arms linked and hearts in sync with the purposes of Heaven. We declare that we will be that glorious bride that You long for when You return. Hallelujah! Amen.*

MY SPIRITUAL PREPARATION FOR TODAY:

_____

_____

_____

_____

_____

DO NOT JUDGE

Judge not, that you be not judged.
—MATTHEW 7:1

WE'VE ALL READ the Book of Job. We know that what happened to Job came from the devil and that the Lord's view of Job was that Job was blameless. We all also know that it was wrong of Job's friends to falsely judge him.

The instinct to judge and criticize without having all the information is rampant in the world. Unfortunately it is also in us, Christ's church.

Could it be that the takeaway message of the Book of Job—the reason it is in the Bible in the first place—is to provide a vivid example that it is wrong to judge without knowing all the facts? Indeed, the Book of Job is a portrait of people with a religious mind-set who are self-assured they are right, who judge without having heard from God.

> O Lord, I don't want to operate out of a religious mind-set, but sometimes that is exactly what I do! My self-assured attitude is the enemy's way of blinding me to my sins. I invite You to come now and strike down the enemy of my soul! I am tired of his manipulative ways. I want to walk in Your ways in every aspect of my life, Jesus. Amen.

MY SPIRITUAL PREPARATION FOR TODAY:

_____

_____

_____

_____

BEWARE THE STRONGHOLD OF COLD LOVE

Because iniquity will abound, the love of many will grow cold.
—MATTHEW 24:12

IS YOUR LOVE growing and becoming softer, brighter, more daring, and more visible? Or is it becoming more discriminating, more calculating, less vulnerable, and less available? This is a very important issue, for your Christianity is only as real as your love. A measurable decrease in your ability to love is evidence that a stronghold of cold love is developing within you.

There is no spiritual unity, and hence no lasting victory, without love. Love is a passion for oneness. Bitterness, on the other hand, is characterized by a noticeable lack of love. This cold love is a demonic stronghold. It shuts down the power of prayer and disables the flow of healing and outreach. In fact, where there is persistent and hardened unforgiveness in a person or church, the demonic world (known in Matthew 18:34, NKJV, as "torturers") has unhindered access.

> *O Father! Hear my heart crying out to You today! I know I have failed in many relationships because of my coldness of heart. Help me to fully understand what unforgiveness means in Your kingdom. I want to stand once again in that place of victory with You, but first I need Your love in me again. I am nothing without Your love. Teach me what true love looks like. Amen.*

MY SPIRITUAL PREPARATION FOR TODAY:

_____

_____

_____

DAY 80

SET CAPTIVES FREE

The Spirit of the Lord GOD is upon me because the LORD has anointed me to preach good news to the poor; He has sent me to heal the broken-hearted, to proclaim liberty to the captives, and the opening of the prison to those who are bound.
—ISAIAH 61:1

WE MUST CRUCIFY our instincts to judge. Of course, there are people who have sinned, who have done things morally and legally wrong. Beloved, I am not saying we should not deal with these problems. If you see criminal action—theft or injustice of some kind that is unmistakably evil—yes, judge by "outer appearance" and inner conviction. Act to bring swift justice. But in most cases these things are not so obvious.

As He has been to us, so we can be to others. We can possess the very same "mind...which was also in Christ Jesus" (Phil. 2:5). Remember, dear friend of God, you are called to follow Christ the Redeemer! Never forget, the heart of Christ is to set captives free.

> *Precious Jesus, forgive me for those times when I reacted with foolish anger and sinful judgment. The next time I see someone I'm tempted to judge, let me be overcome by Your love and compassion for them. In Your mighty name I pray, amen.*

MY SPIRITUAL PREPARATION FOR TODAY:

Offense Robs the Heart

Watching diligently so that no one falls short of the grace of God, lest any root of bitterness spring up to cause trouble, and many become defiled by it.
—Hebrews 12:15

THE SCRIPTURES WARN that even a little root of bitterness springing up in a person's life can defile many. Bitterness is unfulfilled revenge. Another's thoughtlessness or cruelty may have wounded us deeply. It is inevitable that, in a world of increasing harshness and cruelty, we will at some point be hurt. But if we fail to react with love and forgiveness, if we retain in our spirit the debt the offender owes, that offense will rob our hearts of their capacity to love. Imperceptibly we will become a member of the majority of end-time Christians whose love is growing cold.

However, as we embrace God's love and begin to walk in Christlike forgiveness, we are actually pulling down the stronghold of cold love in our lives. Because of this experience, we will soon possess more of the love of Christ than we had previously.

I take all the offenses and hurts and leave them at the foot of the cross. Pull down the stronghold of cold love in my life today. I want Your heart of love, not a useless heart of stone. Thank You, Jesus. Amen.

My spiritual preparation for today:

_____

_____

_____

_____

THE PEACE OF CHRIST

*For nothing is secret that will not be revealed, nor
anything hidden that will not be known and revealed.*
—LUKE 8:17

THE PEACE OF Christ is not just a divine attribute; it is also an organ of communication in the language of God. The Holy Spirit uses peace to communicate with us. If a situation warrants caution, our peace is troubled; if a direction is rightly chosen, peace confirms it. Thus we are admonished by God's Word to let the peace of God rule in our hearts (Col. 3:15). The literal translation for *rule* is "to act as arbiter."

Of course, the "circuitry" that makes our spirit-guidance system accurate is our knowledge of God's Word. We must, therefore, be grounded in God's Word.

When we first were born again, it was not to a religion that we gave our hearts; it was to Christ through the Holy Spirit. The Spirit of God actually entered our lives, and with Him came His inner witness of peace. This is not a little thing, for the gospel is actually called the "gospel of peace" (Eph. 6:15).

O Lord, take me to Your place of peace today, and make me a messenger of the gospel of peace. When my old nature rises up and I am tempted to fall, strengthen me. Come, Holy Spirit; please take up residence in me and never leave. I need You!

MY SPIRITUAL PREPARATION FOR TODAY:

PRESERVING THE QUALITY OF LOVE IN YOUR HEART

If anyone says, "I love God," and hates his brother, he is a liar. For whoever does not love his brother whom he has seen, how can he love God whom he has not seen?
—1 JOHN 4:20

HAVE YOU STUMBLED over someone's weakness or sin lately? Have you gotten back up and continued loving as you did before, or has that fall caused you to withdraw somewhat from walking after love? To preserve the quality of love in your heart, you must forgive those who have caused you to stumble.

Every time you refuse to forgive or fail to overlook a weakness in another, your heart not only hardens toward them, but it also hardens toward God. You cannot form a negative opinion of someone (even though you think they may deserve it!) and allow that opinion to crystallize into an attitude, for every time you do, an aspect of your heart will cool toward God. You may still think you are open to God, but the Scriptures are clear. (See 1 John 4:20.) You may not like what someone has done, but you do not have an option to stop loving them. Love is your only choice.

> *Heavenly Father, sometimes it is so hard for me to love my brother. I allow all sorts of little stones to trip me up. Help me, Father, to forgive and to keep on loving even when someone is unlovable in my eyes. Give me Your eyes to see them. Be the Lord of my heart today. Amen.*

MY SPIRITUAL PREPARATION FOR TODAY:

_____

_____

THE LANGUAGE OF THE SPIRIT

*But the anointing which you have received from Him remains
in you, and you do not need anyone to teach you. For as the
same anointing teaches you concerning all things, and is truth,
and is no lie, and just as it has taught you, remain in Him.*
—1 JOHN 2:27

SOME SAY THAT God doesn't speak to them, but this is not
true. They just haven't learned the language of the Spirit.
When the Holy Spirit comes, He brings communication with
Heaven: dreams, visions, and prophecies all represent union
with God. Therefore you must believe God can get through to
you. What you need is the ability to interpret the influences of
God upon your spirit. To sense what the Spirit of God is saying
to you is, at its essence, the source of true spiritual discernment.

Our goal is to develop that inner witness, for when it is united
with knowledge of the Word of God, we have a powerful resource
added to our arsenal of faith. Remember, the Spirit and the Word
always agree. So if you memorize and study the Word of God
and walk in the Spirit, you will increasingly possess discernment.

> *Holy Spirit, teach me the language of the Spirit so that
> I might receive communication from Heaven! Help me
> to hear God without static or interference. Let my "yes"
> be "yes" and my "no" be "no." Take me to that place
> of abiding where I might stand unhindered in pursuit
> of Your truth. Thank You, precious Holy Spirit. Amen.*

MY SPIRITUAL PREPARATION FOR TODAY:

_____

_____

_____

ACCEPT ONE ANOTHER IN LOVE

That you, being rooted and grounded in love, may be able to...know the love of Christ which surpasses knowledge; that you may be filled with all the fullness of God.
—EPHESIANS 3:17–19

AN EXPERT IN the Law once asked Jesus which was the greatest commandment. His reply was wonderful: "'You shall love the Lord your God with all your heart, and with all your soul, and with all your mind, and with all your strength.' This is the first commandment. The second is this: 'You shall love your neighbor as yourself'" (Mark 12:30–31). Jesus said that the second commandment is like the first. When you love God, your love for others will actually be like your love for God. The more you unconditionally love God, the more you will unconditionally love others.

To those whose attitude is "I am content with just Jesus and me," I say it is wonderful you found Jesus. But you cannot truly have Jesus and simultaneously not do what He says. The outgrowth of love and faith *in* Christ is love and faith *like* Christ's, which means we are committed, even as He is, to His people.

> *Father, I want to be part of the living body of Jesus Christ, not a lifeless appendage. I long to know the fullness of Your love as expressed in Your Son. Shine in my heart today, Lord. Amen.*

MY SPIRITUAL PREPARATION FOR TODAY:

_____

_____

_____

THE ACCUSER OF THE BRETHREN

*Above all things, have unfailing love for one another,
because love covers a multitude of sins. Show hospitality
to one another without complaining. As everyone
has received a gift, even so serve one another with
it, as good stewards of the manifold grace of God.*
—1 PETER 4:8–10

NO ONE OF us is perfect. There will always be issues between Christians that will need godly remedies but not necessarily dismissal. Until Jesus comes, we will have to cover one another and approach correction, when it is necessary, with a gentle spirit.

There is, however, another time when minimal issues or flaws are exaggerated by the enemy to sow strife and division in the church. More churches have been destroyed by the accuser of the brethren and its faultfinding than by either immorality or misuse of church funds. So prevalent is this influence in our society that, among many, faultfinding has been elevated to the status of a "ministry"! The Lord has promised, however, that in His house accusing one another will be replaced with prayer, and fault-finding will be replaced with a love that covers a multitude of sins.

*Dear Jesus, if there is any accusing spirit within me,
remove it quickly and show me how to shut the door
so that it cannot return. Put Yourself as a seal over
my heart, Jesus, so that nothing can abate Your love
to me. Amen.*

MY SPIRITUAL PREPARATION FOR TODAY:

_____

_____

_____

THE DIVINE SOIL OF FAITH AND LOVE

We have all received from His fullness grace upon grace.
—JOHN 1:16

THE HOLY SPIRIT will open up the timeless truths of the Bible; He will also speak to our inner man in dreams, visions, and prophetic words. Yet much of what God reveals must pass through the filter of our degree of purity of heart. Thus, if we will move in true discernment, our view of life must be purged of human thoughts and reactions. We must perceive life through the eyes of Christ.

We will never possess true discernment until we crucify our instincts to judge. Realistically this can take months or even years of uprooting old thought systems that have not been planted in the divine soil of faith and love for people. To appropriate the discernment that is in the "mind of the Lord" (1 Cor. 2:16), we must first find the heart of Christ. The heart and love of Jesus is summed up in His own words: "I did not come to judge the world, but to save the world" (John 12:47).

> *Dear Jesus, I give You permission to uproot all old thoughts that have set themselves up against my knowledge of You. Replace the old soil of my heart with Your divine soil so that Your grace may abound in me. Amen.*

MY SPIRITUAL PREPARATION FOR TODAY:

_____

_____

_____

_____

Day 88

The Smoke Screen of a Critical Spirit

For in Christ Jesus neither circumcision nor uncircumcision
means anything, but faith which works through love.
—Galatians 5:6

THE FAULTFINDER SPIRIT's assignment is to assault relationships on all levels. It attacks families, churches, and inter-
church associations, seeking to bring irreparable schisms into our
unity. Masquerading as discernment, this spirit will slip into our
opinions of other people; it will leave us critical and judgmental.

The people who are held captive by this deceitful spirit
become "crusaders." In many cases the things they deem wrong
or lacking are the very areas in which the Lord seeks to position them for intercession. What might otherwise be an opportunity for spiritual growth becomes an occasion of stumbling
and withdrawal. In truth, their criticisms are a smoke screen for
a prayerless heart and an unwillingness to serve. Consequently
we all need to evaluate our attitude toward others. If our
thoughts are other than faith working through love (Gal. 5:6),
we need to be aware that we may be under spiritual attack.

> *O Jesus, Your great sacrifice for me is more than I*
> *can comprehend. That You would die for me while I*
> *was still a sinner! How can this be, and yet it is! For-*
> *give me for all those times I thought myself clever and*
> *spiritual when rooting out the faults of others. I am*
> *so in need of You. Stay by my side today, Jesus. Amen.*

MY SPIRITUAL PREPARATION FOR TODAY:

_____

_____

_____

BECOMING MORE LIKE CHRIST

*Let all bitterness, wrath, anger, outbursts, and
blasphemies, with all malice, be taken away from you.
And be kind one to another, tenderhearted, forgiving
one another, just as God in Christ also forgave you.*
—EPHESIANS 4:31–32

JESUS PREPARED HIS disciples to be proactive in their forgiveness. Using Himself as their example, He taught, "Everyone who speaks a word against the Son of Man will be forgiven" (Luke 12:10). Jesus prepared His heart to forgive men before they ever sinned against Him. He knew His mission was to die for men, not condemn them.

Likewise we are called to His mission as well. We are called to die that others may live. Therefore we must realize that before our perception develops, our love must mature until our normal attitude is one of forgiveness.

> *Jesus, I fall so short of Your example. Help me to forgive people in advance, to have a predetermined mind-set of forgiveness. Search my heart for any traces of unforgiveness, and teach me to die to myself that others might know You. Amen.*

MY SPIRITUAL PREPARATION FOR TODAY:

_____

_____

_____

_____

_____

THE FAULTFINDING SPIRIT

Jesus said… "The scribes and the Pharisees sit in Moses'
seat. Therefore, whatever they tell you to observe, that
observe and do, but do not do their works. For they
speak, but do nothing. They fasten heavy loads that are
hard to carry and lay them on men's shoulders, but they
themselves will not move them with their finger."
—MATTHEW 23:1–4

A S I MENTIONED on Day 86, more churches are destroyed
by the accuser of the brethren and its faultfinding than by
immorality or misuse of church funds. When this spirit infil-
trates an individual's mind, its accusations come with such
venom and intimidation that even those who should know
better are bewildered and then seduced by its influence. Nearly
all involved take their eyes off Jesus and focus upon "issues,"
ignoring during the contention that Jesus is actually praying for
His body to become one.

Beguiled by this demon, accusations and counteraccusations
rifle through the soul of the congregation, stimulating suspicion
and fear among the people. Weariness and devastation wrack
the targeted ministry, while discouragement blankets servants of
God. Brethren, the spirit behind such accusations must be dis-
cerned, for its motive is not to restore and heal but to destroy.

Heavenly Father, let me hear and discern when the
accuser of the brethren is moving against the people
of God in my sphere of influence that I might stand
firm in the face of the accuser. Amen.

MY SPIRITUAL PREPARATION FOR TODAY:

_____

_____

WALKING IN REPENTANCE

Why do you see the speck that is in your brother's eye, but do not consider the plank that is in your own eye? Or how will you say to your brother, "Let me pull the speck out of your eye," when a log is in your own eye? You hypocrite! First take the plank out of your own eye, and then you will see clearly to take the speck out of your brother's eye.
—MATTHEW 7:3–5

REPENTANCE IS THE removal of the "logs" within our vision; it is the true beginning of seeing clearly. There are many who suppose they are receiving the Lord's discernment concerning one thing or another. Perhaps in some things they are; only God knows. But many are simply judging others and calling it discernment. Jesus commands us to judge not.

If you seek to have a heart that does not condemn, you must truly crucify the instinct to judge. Then you will have laid a true foundation for the gift of discernment, for you will have prepared your heart to receive dreams, visions, and insights from God. You will be unstained by human bias and corruption.

Dear Lord, forgive me for those times when I judged others when what I saw in them was really a reflection of my own brokenness. Thank You for forgiving me. Teach me how to forgive others. Amen.

MY SPIRITUAL PREPARATION FOR TODAY:

_____

_____

_____

_____

BEWARE LOVELESS CORRECTION

*Now if your brother sins against you, go and tell him his
fault between you and him alone. If he listens to you, you
have gained your brother. But if he does not listen, then
take with you one or two others, that by the testimony of
two or three witnesses every word may be established.*
—MATTHEW 18:15–16

NEARLY EVERY BELIEVER has faced the assault of the faultfinder spirit at one time or another. Each has known the
depression of trying to track down this accusing spirit as it whispers its gossip through the local church: trusted friends seem
distant, established relationships are shaken, and the vision of
the church is in a quagmire of strife and inaction.

To mask the diabolical nature of its activity, the faultfinder
spirit will often garb its criticisms in religious clothing. Under the
pretense of protecting sheep from a "gnat-sized" error in doctrine,
it forces the flock to swallow a "camel-sized" error of loveless correction. Where is the "spirit of meekness" of which Paul speaks in
Galatians 6:1, the humility in "watching yourselves, lest you also
be tempted"? Where is the love motive to "restore such a one"?

> *Father, I pray today for the body of Christ, of which
> I am a part, to come into a place of repentance for
> behaving in violation of Scripture. So often we act
> like sheep without a shepherd when You are there,
> waiting patiently for us to step back onto Your path
> that leads to abundant life. Amen.*

MY SPIRITUAL PREPARATION FOR TODAY:

_____

_____

THE RIGHT RESPONSE

*For it is shameful even to speak of those things
which are done by them in secret. But all things
are exposed when they are revealed by the light,
for everything that becomes visible is light.*
—EPHESIANS 5:12–13

IN ORDER TO discern, you cannot react. To perceive, you must make yourself blind to what seems apparent. People may react to you, but you cannot react to them. You must always remain forgiving in nature, for the demons you cast out will challenge you, masquerading as the very voice of the person you seek to deliver. You must discern the difference between the oppressing spirit and the person oppressed.

Should God reveal to us the hearts of men and then call us to release them from captivity, we cannot react to what they say. As our perception becomes more like Christ Himself and the secrets of men's hearts are revealed to us, we cannot even react to what they think. We are called to navigate the narrow and well-hidden path into the true nature of men's needs. If we would truly help men, we must remember we are following a Lamb.

Father, help me to respond to the needs and hidden thoughts and motives of others with Your love and mercy. Let everything I do draw others closer to You and reveal Your heart to them. Amen.

MY SPIRITUAL PREPARATION FOR TODAY:

_____

_____

_____

DAY 94

THE PURE EXAMPLE

Those whom I love, I rebuke and discipline.
Therefore be zealous and repent.
—REVELATION 3:19

THE MINISTRY OF reproof must be patterned after Christ and not the accuser of the brethren. When Jesus corrected the churches in Asia (Rev. 2–3), He positioned His rebuke between praise and promises. He reassured the churches that the voice about to expose their sin was the very voice that inspired their virtue. After encouraging them, He then brought correction.

Is this not His way with each of us? Even in the most serious corrections, the voice of Jesus is always the embodiment of "grace and truth" (John 1:14). Jesus said of the sheep, "They know his voice. Yet they will never follow a stranger, but will run away from him" (John 10:4–5). Remember, if the word of rebuke or correction does not offer grace for restoration, it is not the voice of your Shepherd. If you are one of Christ's sheep, you will flee from it.

Heavenly Father, thank You that the arms of Jesus my Shepherd wait for me. Lead me to that place between my Savior's praises and promises that I might find Your godly correction and taste the abundant life You have for me. Amen.

MY SPIRITUAL PREPARATION FOR TODAY:

_____

_____

_____

_____

LEARNING TO LISTEN

*But He said, "Indeed, blessed are those who
hear the word of God and keep it."*
—LUKE 11:28

THE LORD DESIRES we learn how to wait and listen for His voice. He draws our focus to His unlimited power and admonishes us, "Be still and know that I am God" (Ps. 46:10). We cannot engage in spiritual warfare without first becoming conscious of, and submitted to, God. It is through Him that we gain insight into the activity of the enemy. All true discernment comes through a heart that has ceased striving, a heart that knows, even in the fiery trial of its personal struggle, that the Lord is God.

If what you have to say to someone is very important, you will require their undivided attention. With few exceptions, so also the Holy Spirit does not speak to us until we slow down, tune out the static, and give Him our heart in focused attention. To walk in true discernment, we must be quiet before God. We must learn how to listen.

> *Father, I come before You now, tuning out the static and giving my full attention to You. Give me patience to wait upon You until my heart hears Your voice. I want to draw away to that secret place in the sweet presence of my Lord. Amen.*

MY SPIRITUAL PREPARATION FOR TODAY:

_____

_____

_____

DIVINE FORGETFULNESS

Their sins and their lawless deeds will I remember no more.
—HEBREWS 10:17

SATAN SEEKS NOT only to accuse us as individuals but also to blend into our minds criticisms and condemnation against others as well. Instead of praying for one another, we react in the flesh against offenses. Our un-Christlike responses are then easily manipulated by the accusing spirit. Therefore we cast down the accuser of the brethren by learning to *pray for* one another instead of *preying on* one another. We must learn to forgive in the same manner as Christ has forgiven us. If one has repented of his sins, we must exercise the same attitude of "divine forgetfulness" that exists in Heaven. We defeat the fault-finder when we emulate the nature of Jesus: as a lamb Christ died for sinners; as a priest He intercedes.

> *Dear Lord, I am guilty of preying on others instead of praying for them. I repent now in Your holy presence and look to the finished work of the cross for the righteousness bought at such a price for me and for all. Thank You, Jesus. Amen.*

MY SPIRITUAL PREPARATION FOR TODAY:

_____

_____

_____

_____

_____

_____

ABOUNDING LOVE

*And this I pray, that your love may abound yet more
and more in knowledge and in all discernment.*
—PHILIPPIANS 1:9

DISCERNMENT COMES FROM abounding love. What is abounding love? It is love that leaps out from us toward others. It is motivated by long-term commitment; it is anointed by sacrificial charity. There is a false discernment that is based on mistrust, suspicion, and fear. You can recognize false discernment by the coldness around it. False discernment may be packaged in a type of love, but it does not originate in love; it comes out of criticism. True discernment is rooted deeply in love.

False discernment sees the outside of the person or situation and pretends it knows the inside. Godly discernment comes from having godly motives; godly motives are those rooted in God's committed love. In like manner our capacity to discern the needs of the church will never rise higher than that which is superficial if we do not know Christ's heart for His people.

*Lord, I need new eyes to see as You see. I need eyes
that see through the lens of Your love. I want the kind
of love that rejoices with the truth that is in Your heart
for each person. I can't do this without You. Come
and take up all the space in my heart today. Amen.*

MY SPIRITUAL PREPARATION FOR TODAY:

_____

_____

_____

_____

GOD'S ANSWER FOR PAIN

I will give you a new heart, and a new spirit I will put
within you. And I will take away the stony heart out
of your flesh, and I will give you a heart of flesh.
—EZEKIEL 36:26

BITTERNESS IS THE most visible symptom of the stronghold of cold love. To deal with cold love, we must repent and forgive the one who hurt us. Painful experiences are allowed by God to teach us how to love our enemies. Our character is tested by the way we respond and handle these experiences. If we still have unforgiveness toward someone, we have failed this test. Fortunately it was just a test, not a final exam.

We actually need to thank God for the opportunity to grow in divine love. Thank Him that your whole life is not being swallowed up in bitterness and resentment. Millions of souls are swept off into eternal judgment every day without any hope of escaping from embitterment, but you have been given God's answer for your pain. God gives you a way out: love!

> *Father, let nothing rob my heart of Your love today.*
> *I take whatever bitterness is in my heart and give*
> *it to You. Help me to walk in forgiveness today and*
> *every day. Amen.*

MY SPIRITUAL PREPARATION FOR TODAY:

_____

_____

_____

_____

_____

A TRANQUIL AND PURE HEART

Blessed are the pure in heart, for they shall see God.
—MATTHEW 5:8

LIFE, AS WE perceive it, is based upon the condition of our hearts. This is very important because the gifts of the Spirit must pass through our hearts before they are presented to the world around us. In other words, if our hearts are not right, the gifts will not be right either. When the heart has unrest, it cannot hear from God. Therefore we must learn to mistrust our judgment when our hearts ares bitter, angry, ambitious, or harboring strife for any reason. The Scriptures tell us to let the peace of God rule in our hearts (Col. 3:15). To hear clearly from God, we must first have peace.

> *Lord, I come to You like the psalmist and say, "Create in me a clean heart, O God, and renew a right spirit within me. Do not cast me away from Your presence, or do not take Your Holy Spirit from me. Restore to me the joy of Your salvation, and uphold me with Your willing spirit" (Ps. 51:10–13). Amen.*

MY SPIRITUAL PREPARATION FOR TODAY:

_____

_____

_____

_____

_____

_____

_____

PERSECUTION: A DEED OF THE FLESH

But as it was then, he who was born after the flesh persecuted
him who was born after the Spirit, so it is now also.
—GALATIANS 4:29

SADLY IT IS often leaders who have fallen from the intensity of their first love for Christ who become the fiercest persecutors of others who are seeking to possess more of the Holy Spirit. Persecution is a deed of the flesh.

To combat this enemy, we must create an atmosphere of grace among us as individuals and between us as churches. Like the Father who has given us life, we must seek to cause all things to work together for good. If one stumbles, we must be quick to cover him, without going so far as to create a false "cover-up" where we actually condone sin or hypocrisy. Love finds a redemptive way to cover a multitude of sins.

> *Heavenly Father, teach me how to operate in a culture of honor toward my brothers and sisters in Christ, just as I would want them to treat me honorably even in the midst of my sin. Amen.*

MY SPIRITUAL PREPARATION FOR TODAY:

_____

_____

_____

_____

_____

_____

Trust the Spirit's Guidance

*Immediately, when Jesus perceived in His spirit that they
so reasoned within themselves, He said to them, "Why
do you comtemplate these things in your hearts?"*
—Mark 2:8

Scripture says that Jesus "perceived in His spirit" the thoughts and motives of others (Mark 2:8). The discernment we want to develop is a spiritual thing, not soulish—and definitely not something borrowed from the occult.

Let's put this into perspective: we have an inner witness that gives us peace while helping us decide and discern. This "peace connection" does not, however, allow us to ignore input from leaders or others whom God may use. While we must maintain sovereignty over our will, God gives us ministries to train and equip us (Eph. 4:11–12). That said, it is the anointing of the Holy Spirit that is the final amen to the truth of God.

Coupled with the Word of God, your radar can be a type of scanner that actually discerns hidden issues or danger. Thus you can trust the Holy Spirit's guidance to help you recognize what may be troubling you in your spirit.

> *Jesus, I need more of Your peace today. I know that
> it will make the power of discernment more effective
> in my life. I ask for You to lead and guide me and
> give me an inner witness that I am on the right path.
> In Your name, amen.*

My spiritual preparation for today:

_____

_____

_____

A SEASON OF PRUNING

Every branch that bears fruit, He prunes,
that it may bear more fruit.
—JOHN 15:2

DURING A TIME of pruning God requires new levels of surrender as well as a fresh crucifixion of the flesh. It is often a time of humiliation, testing, and seeming ineffectiveness as God deepens our dependency upon Him. Unfortunately it frequently occurs before the church and before principalities and powers. The faultfinder spirit and those who have come to think as it thinks find in their target's vulnerability an opportunity to crush him.

What would otherwise have become an incubator of life becomes a coffin of death. Those who might otherwise emerge with the clarity and power of prophetic vision are beaten down and abandoned, cut off from the very people who should have prayed them through to resurrection. Today God is seeking to raise up His servants with increased power and authority. In the pruning stage of their growth will we water their dryness with prayer and encouragement, or will we be vultures drawn to devour their dying flesh?

> *Father! Protect me in the time of pruning from those who would be used by the accuser to bring me down in my vulnerability. Crucify my flesh afresh that I might surrender all to You, and use me to provide prayer and encouragement to those around me when they are dry and in need of refreshing. In Jesus's name, amen.*

MY SPIRITUAL PREPARATION FOR TODAY:

_____

_____

DIVISION IN THE BODY

He who does not gather with Me scatters abroad.
—MATTHEW 12:30

THIS SCATTERING, DIVIDING process among the Lord's sheep has gone on long enough. Jesus has set His heart to bring healing and unity to His body. In this regard, through the prophet Jeremiah, the Lord spoke a somber warning. He said, "Woe to the shepherds who destroy and scatter the sheep of My pasture!" (Jer. 23:1) The Son of God is not pleased with the carnal divisions in His body! Indeed, the Lord promises to chasten those pastors who continue to build their kingdoms without laboring together to build His. To them He says, "I am about to punish you for the evil of your deeds" (v. 2).

> Lord, forgive us our sins. We are a stiff-necked people given over to division and strife far too easily. Come and purify my heart today that I might stand in the place of the righteous and not the sinner. Show me how to lead by example in my own church today. Put Your love in my heart yet again, precious Lord. Amen.

MY SPIRITUAL PREPARATION FOR TODAY:

_____

_____

_____

_____

_____

_____

_____

THE MEASURE OF CHRISTLIKE MATURITY

Let this mind be in you all, which was also in Christ Jesus.
—PHILIPPIANS 2:5

THAT SOMEONE SHOULD discover the imperfections of their pastor or church is by no means a sign of spirituality. Indeed, we could find fault with the church even before we were Christians. There is a difference between a self-righteous, critical spirit and the grace and truth of the Holy Spirit. What we do with what we see, however, is the measure of Christlike maturity. Remember, when Jesus saw the condition of mankind, He identified with humanity, took the form of man, and then died for our sins (Phil. 2:7–8). He didn't condemn us; He died for us. Paul's admonition is that we have the attitude or the mind-set in ourselves "which was also in Christ Jesus" (v. 5).

> *Lord, forgive me for confusing a critical spirit with discernment. Let the grace and truth of the Spirit fill my life so completely that it overflows in my actions toward my pastor and others in my church. Amen.*

MY SPIRITUAL PREPARATION FOR TODAY:

_____

_____

_____

_____

_____

_____

COMMITTED TO REDEEM

I will gather the remnant of My flock...and they
shall be fruitful and increase. I will also set up
shepherds over them who will feed them; and
they will fear no more, nor be dismayed.
—JEREMIAH 23:3–4

TRUE CORRECTION WILL proceed with reverence, not revenge. For to be anointed with Christ's authority to rebuke, we must be committed to men with Christ's goal to redeem. But if we are angry, embittered, or jealous toward another, we cannot even pray correctly for that person, much less reprove him.

Jesus, the great Lion of Judah, was declared worthy to bring forth judgment by virtue of His nature: He was a Lamb slain for men's sin. If we are not determined to die for men, we have no right to judge them.

> *O Lord, let me die to self today. I know You do not intend this life to be all about me, but too often that is exactly what my life is. Please come and grow my heart so that it has room for others. I don't want to be judged by others, and I truly don't want to give in to a judgmental spirit toward others, but too often that is what I do. I need a makeover, Lord! Make me over today in Your image so that I can bless the one in front of me. Amen.*

MY SPIRITUAL PREPARATION FOR TODAY:

_____

_____

_____

Day 106

Repair the Breach

*You have not gone up into the gaps, nor did you
build up the hedge for the house of Israel to
stand in the battle on the day of the Lord.*
—Ezekiel 13:5

GOD NEEDS PEOPLE who, when they see a gap in the church
wall, will go up into the breaches and rebuild the wall so that
the church will stand in the day of battle. But will you do that?

Without a hint of pride you will seek ways to be a blessing to
other churches. Your Christlike love will cast out fears. You will
sincerely have a burden to see the entire body of Christ brought
forth, not just your local assembly; you will respect the diversity
of ways through which Christ reveals Himself in the church.

Do not expect to teach or lead, but to love and serve. In this,
God is not looking for leaders but followers of the Lord Jesus
Christ. The breaches between us must be filled, and we must
learn to stand together in the day of the Lord.

> *Father, take any and every hint of pride from me today
> and cast it into the deepest part of the sea. I don't want
> to be prideful. Give me a heart burdened for the whole
> church. Take me to those places in Your Word where
> Jesus gives examples of what it truly means to live and
> operate with a servant's heart, and seal them on my
> heart so that serving others becomes the first thing I
> think of, not the last. Thank You, Father. Amen.*

My spiritual preparation for today:

_____

_____

_____

SPEAK IN LOVE AND HUMILITY

Let your speech always be with grace, seasoned with salt,
that you may know how you should answer everyone.
—COLOSSIANS 4:6

THE LORD'S WORD to us is that in the house of the Lord criticism must be replaced with prayer and faultfinding eliminated with a covering of love. Where there is error, we must go with a motive to restore. Where there are wrong doctrines, let us maintain a gentle spirit as we seek to correct those in opposition.

> *Lord Jesus, forgive us for our lack of prayer and the weakness of our love. Master, we want to be like You, that when we see a need, instead of criticizing, we lay down our lives for it. Lord, deliver Your church of this demonic faultfinding spirit! In Jesus's name, amen.*

MY SPIRITUAL PREPARATION FOR TODAY:

_____

_____

_____

_____

_____

_____

_____

_____

_____

_____

CALLED TO STAND IN THE GAP

*Your kingdom come; Your will be done
on earth, as it is in heaven.*
—MATTHEW 6:10

YOU DO NOT need skill to find fault. But if you want to be like Christ, you have to be willing to lay your life down for people's sins. You have to be an intercessor who "stands in the gap." *The "gap" is the distance between the way things are and the way things should be.* You stand in that space, cast down the accuser of the brethren, and intercede! Have you seen something that is wrong? It is only because Jesus wants you to stand in the gap and pray to see it changed.

Let us lay down our lives in committed faith, believing that in our lifetimes, on this earth and in our communities, the corporate church of Jesus Christ will be restored, united, and made ready as a bride for her Beloved!

> *Lord, I want to stand today, ready to do Your will. Find me on my knees, Father, praying to raise up the age-old foundations. Let me be counted among the peacemakers today, the sons and daughters of God who bring healing, honor, and order to Your church. Find me worthy today, Lord. Find me worthy. Amen.*

MY SPIRITUAL PREPARATION FOR TODAY:

_____

_____

_____

_____

_____

GUARD YOUR HEART

Hear, my son, and be wise; and guide your heart in the way.
—PROVERBS 23:19

WHAT IS IT then that can worm into an individual's thought life, burrow into his heart, and then grow so compelling that he is willing to risk everything he's loved and attained for a mere fulfillment of the flesh? Is it just sin? Or is there something deeper—a lack of spiritual discernment—that left the heart of that person vulnerable to demonic manipulation? Perhaps their heart was unguarded to the exploitation of hell.

Please note that I am not blaming the devil for every sin we commit. The fact is, selfishness and self-indulgence, which produce sin, are basic instincts of our fallen nature. At the same time let us also discern the unique warfare of our times. Our world has been flooded with hyper-sexuality and excess. The "red-light district" has moved from the city and entered our homes via the Internet, movies, and television. We deceive ourselves if we think we can accommodate an immoral imagination and it not contaminate how we act out our lives. We each must learn to guard our hearts in all things and at all times lest the devil come in through an open door and proceed to tear our house down.

> *Father, the possibilities for sin today are no different than they were two thousand years ago; they are just packaged differently. Give me the discernment I need, and thank You for providing Jesus, my way out of temptation. Amen.*

MY SPIRITUAL PREPARATION FOR TODAY:

_____

_____

DAY 110

WORSHIP IN THE WILDERNESS

But You are holy, O You who inhabits the praises of Israel.
—PSALM 22:3

YOU WILL REMEMBER that when Moses first spoke of God's loving concern, we read that the Hebrews "bowed down and worshipped" (Exod. 4:31). But when trials and pressures came, they fell quickly into murmuring, complaining, and blatant rebellion. Their worship was superficial, self-serving, and conditional—a form without a heart of worship.

Indeed, the Lord's purpose with Israel in the wilderness was to perfect true worship, which is based upon the reality of God, not circumstances. The Lord knows that the heart that will worship Him in the wilderness of affliction will continue to worship in the promised land of plenty.

> *Almighty God, teach me what it means to worship based on the reality of who You are, not on my current circumstances. Find me on my knees in the wilderness today with songs of praise on my lips! Hallelujah! Amen.*

MY SPIRITUAL PREPARATION FOR TODAY:

CONFRONT THE BATTLE HONESTLY

*Therefore put to death the parts of your earthly nature:
sexual immorality, uncleanness, inordinate affection,
evil desire, and covetousness, which is idolatry.*
—**COLOSSIANS 3:5**

AN UNGUARDED MIND that willfully harbors darkness will
have spiritual predators cultivating and probing its moral
weaknesses. Indeed, through modern technology an alternate
reality—a fantasy world created by our mind's imagination—
can be created and accessed by the demonic realm.

There is much within the fallen human nature that can be
exploited and plundered for evil. When we do not guard our
hearts and avoid what is sinful, this fantasy realm unfolds into
darkness, leaving our thought processes open and unprotected
against demons that build strongholds in the human soul.

Listen well: what entertains us actually *enters* us. If you are
entertained by pornography or sexual fantasy, perverse or cor-
rupt thoughts, you are opening your soul to hell. You must confront this battle honestly, repent, and set a guard over your heart.

> *Heavenly Father, deliver me from evil today. I con-
> fess that I am weak and in need of Your Holy Spirit's
> power in my life today to overcome the wiles of the
> enemy. Come and wash me clean, and help me to
> sin no more. Amen.*

MY SPIRITUAL PREPARATION FOR TODAY:

_____

_____

_____

"ALTAR" YOUR PAST

Forgetting those things which are behind and reaching forward to those things which are ahead, I press toward the goal to the prize of the high calling of God in Christ Jesus.
—PHILIPPIANS 3:13–14

WHAT WE CALL *memory* is actually our spirit gazing at the substance of our soul. With few exceptions those events that we remember the most have also shaped us the most. Our reaction to each event, whether that event was positive or negative, is poured into the creative marrow of our individuality, where it is blended into the nature of our character. Indeed, the reason our natural minds cannot forget certain incidents is because those events have literally become part of our nature.

When Scripture commands us to forget "those things which are behind," it is saying we must undo the consequences that have come from our un-Christlike reactions. With God this is not impossible, *for although the events of our lives are irreversible, our reactions to those events can still be changed.* As our wrong reactions to the past change, we change. In other words, although we cannot alter the past, we can put our past upon the "altar" as an act of worship.

> *Dear Lord, I give You my past. I place it on the altar and with Your help, may I never pick it back up. Thank You for restoring my soul. Let me go forward with a new focus and a new mind that is willing and able to forget what lies behind. Amen.*

MY SPIRITUAL PREPARATION FOR TODAY:

_____

_____

DIVINELY POWERFUL WEAPONS

*And since they did not see fit to acknowledge
God, God gave them over to a debased mind, to
do those things which are not proper.*
—ROMANS 1:28

ONE MAY ARGUE, "My battle is just sin, not warfare." Perhaps that is true for you, but for others it is a spiritual attack on an unguarded heart. Its power may be aimed at Christians in general, but its specific target is church leaders and those called to places of authority in God's kingdom.

For those in the kingdom of God, "the weapons of our warfare are…mighty through God" (2 Cor. 10:4). Our weapons and defenses are mighty, but we must use them. We cannot be casual with sin or temptation. Don't feed your sexual appetites, for these kinds of addictions only go from bad to worse (Rom. 1:24–28).

> *O Father, I confess that I have sinned against You with my thought life and at times even with my physical body. I have failed to guard my heart, and I allowed addiction to take root. I repent now of my sins and ask for Your forgiveness. Wash me clean and give the wherewithal to stay clean and pure of thought and action in Your sight. In Jesus's name, amen.*

MY SPIRITUAL PREPARATION FOR TODAY:

_____

_____

_____

_____

REFRESHING WATER

*But whoever drinks of the water that I shall give him will
never thirst. Indeed, the water that I shall give him will
become in him a well of water springing up into eternal life.*
—JOHN 4:14

PSALM 84 EXPRESSES in praise to God the wonderful effect
worship has upon the soul. "Blessed is the man whose
strength is in You, in whose heart are the paths to Zion. As
they pass through the Valley of Baca [weeping], they make it a
spring; the early rain also covers it with pools" (vv. 5–6).

If you "continually praise" God (v. 4), your worship of God
will transform the negative assault of the enemy into "a well" of
sweet refreshing waters. No matter what befalls a worshipper,
their valley of weeping always becomes a spring covered with
blessings. You cannot successfully engage in warfare or pass
safely through the wilderness of this life without first becoming
a worshipper of God.

> *Lord, let today be a day when the praise on my lips
> lifts me out of this valley of weeping into Your spring
> of sweet refreshing water. I want to be like a child
> today, dancing in the rain of Your presence. Praise
> Your holy name!*

MY SPIRITUAL PREPARATION FOR TODAY:

_____

_____

_____

_____

_____

PERFECTLY SURRENDERED

Let the high praises of God be in their mouths,
and two-edged swords in their hands.
—PSALM 149:6

IN THESE CLOSING moments of this age the Lord will have a people whose purpose for living is to please God with their lives. They are His worshippers. They are on earth only to please God, and when He is pleased, they also are pleased.

One would think that God would protect them, guarding them in such a way that they would not be marred. Instead they are marred more than others. Indeed, the Lord seems pleased to crush them, putting them to grief. For in the midst of their physical and emotional pain their loyalty to Christ grows pure and perfect. And in the face of persecutions their love and worship toward God become all-consuming.

Would that all Christ's servants were so perfectly surrendered. Yet God finds His pleasure in us all. But as the days of the kingdom draw near and the warfare at the end of this age increases, those who have been created solely for the worship of God will come forth in the power and glory of the Son.

> *Father God, help me to see my pain and conflicts with new eyes—as chances to exude a deeper and purer worship that only comes from total surrender to You. Let my life be a sweet-smelling fragrance before Your throne. I give myself wholly to You. In Jesus's name, amen.*

MY SPIRITUAL PREPARATION FOR TODAY:

_____

_____

CONDITIONED IN THE WILDERNESS

The LORD your God is He who goes over
before you as a consuming fire.
—DEUTERONOMY 9:3

JOSHUA HAD ALREADY known the Lord in a wonderful, inti-mate way in the wilderness tabernacle when, in Joshua 5:13, the Lord revealed Himself to Joshua in a new way. The Son of God Himself had come as Captain of the Host to lead His people into war.

Though initially Joshua was taken aback, both Joshua and the people with him were more prepared for this battle than they realized. Their time in the wilderness had conditioned them for war.

Likewise the wilderness for you has not been a time of pun-ishment but a season of preparation and of learning obedience. You have watched in fear the decline and spiritual death of others who repeatedly disobeyed the Lord. But you have not stumbled over their disobedience; you have learned from it. Today you walk in the fear of God and are not blinded by the sin of presumption.

Dear God, I thank You that even times in the wilder-
ness are not wasted with You. I am more prepared
now for battle than I think I am. Let Your resurrection
power begin afresh the work of holiness in me. Amen.

MY SPIRITUAL PREPARATION FOR TODAY:

An idea that is taken to be
true + often used as the basis
for other ideas, although it is
not known
for certain.

STRENGTH FOR THE BATTLE

THE POWER OF THE KINGDOM

Now the salvation and the power and the kingdom of
our God and the authority of His Christ have come, for
the accuser of our brothers... has been cast down.
—REVELATION 12:10

JESUS CALLS US beyond the standards of "church as usual"; He calls us to reveal the life and power of the kingdom of God. What is the difference between the church and God's kingdom? Those who seek first for God's kingdom are love-motivated people who are given to prayer. When they see a need, instead of judging, they intercede.

There will be an actual point in time when the "salvation and the power and the kingdom of our God," as well as the "authority of His Christ," are manifested in the earth. While we wait patiently for the fulfillment of that glorious event, the spirit of this eternal reality can be possessed any time a people determine to walk free of criticism and faultfinding and turn their sights toward purity, love, and prayer for each other.

> *Heavenly Father, let me be found walking free of criticism and faultfinding today, with my eyes fixed on You. Let Your love abound in my heart and in my prayers. I love Your presence. Fill me up to over-flowing today. Amen.*

MY SPIRITUAL PREPARATION FOR TODAY:

_____

_____

_____

_____

Taking the Next Steps

Because he has set his love upon Me, threfore I will deliver him; I will set him on high, because he has known My name.
—Psalm 91:14

IF YOU ARE currently in bondage to sin, as powerful as the sin seems, the enemy will also work to isolate your battle from others. The efforts we spend hiding sin are the very tools Satan uses to entrap us in it; so talk to someone (Eph. 5:11–13). If you have a history of sin, then begin a process of cleansing, of washing your "robes…in the blood of the Lamb" (Rev. 7:14). Confess your sins one by one to God and one another.

Now is a good time to build yourself up spiritually. Take the next step in your spiritual journey. Get back in the Word, for it is the sword of the Spirit. Use the authority of God's Word to defend your heart against spiritual attacks.

The most important thing you can do is to return wholeheartedly to God. Beloved, it is time to set a guard over your heart.

> *Lord God, this day I humble myself before Your throne. You see my heart and the battle I have faced. I ask that You restore me; make me wiser. Let not my enemy triumph over me. Fill me with Your Holy Spirit, and grant me the grace to walk with a pure heart, a guarded heart, before You. In Jesus's name, amen.*

MY SPIRITUAL PREPARATION FOR TODAY:

_____

_____

_____

_____

THE PLACE OF INTERCESSION

Therefore He is able to save to the uttermost those who come to God through Him, because He at all times lives to make intercession for them.
—HEBREWS 7:25

IF WE SEE a need in the body of Christ, our first reaction should be to intercede and not simply criticize. Our pattern must be to follow Christ in building and restoring, not to echo the accuser of the brethren in merely finding fault.

You see, we will always be serving in churches where things are wrong. Our response to what we see defines how Christlike we are actually becoming. If we see weakness in the body of Christ, our call is to supply strength. If we see sin, our response is to be an example of virtue. When we discover fear, we must impart courage, and where there is worldliness, we must display holiness. Our call is to enter the place of intercession and stand there until the body of Christ is built up in that area.

> *Dear Lord, anoint me with Your redemptive motives today so that I might take my place in intercession. Use me to supply strength, courage, and holiness at all times. In Jesus's name I pray, amen.*

MY SPIRITUAL PREPARATION FOR TODAY:

_____

_____

_____

_____

_____

The Lord's Strategy

*Therefore be imitators of God as
beloved children. Walk in love.*
—Ephesians 5:1–2

Remember, God's will requires us to become Christ-like. To facilitate His purpose, God allows whatever is not Christlike within us to remain vulnerable to spiritual assault. While we take authority over the spirit of witchcraft (or any other spirit) and renounce the effects of its curse, we must also become aggressive in our love. We are not warring against individuals but against the spirits that enslave them. We cannot overcome evil with evil; we must overcome evil with love.

> *Father, help me to remember that I am warring against spirits of the enemy, not against any individual or group of people. These people need You, God, and they need to be delivered from the spirits that bind them. Help me to be Your weapon in the battle that frees them. The battle belongs to You; I cannot do it in my own strength. Thank You, Jesus!*

My spiritual preparation for today:

_____

_____

_____

_____

_____

_____

AT THE THRONE OF GRACE

What you have said in the darkness will be heard in the light.
—LUKE 12:3

STUDY THE BOOK of Revelation, and in the description of God's throne you will find no devil there. Investigate Hebrews chapter 12, and in the discourse concerning the heavenly Jerusalem, again you will see no devil in Heaven. How then do we explain the scriptures that allude to a devil in Heaven?

If it is true that the devil is not in the highest Heaven, how then does he accuse the saints before the throne of God? Although the devil does not have immediate access to God, he does have access to our thoughts and words. When we harbor sympathetic attitudes toward faultfinding, when we justify gossip and negative criticism, we are actually giving Satan the use of our mouths to accuse the saints before God! We must realize that "all things are bare and exposed to the eyes of Him to whom we must give account" (Heb. 4:13). God, who is light, indeed hears the voice of the accuser, even in the guarded confidences spoken to a spouse or friend.

> O Father, save me from unwittingly becoming an instrument of Satan! Teach me how to put a governor on my thoughts and my words so that all my thoughts and utterances are pleasing to You. Lay bare before me those things that are in me that hurt Your heart so that I may deliver them up to Your throne for disposal. Throw them on the trash heap, Lord! Give me strength for today. Amen.

MY SPIRITUAL PREPARATION FOR TODAY:

_____

_____

IN HIS LIKENESS

But refuse profane and foolish myths. Instead,
exercise in the ways of godliness.
—1 TIMOTHY 4:7

GOD CANNOT ESTABLISH within us a pure heart and a steadfast spirit without allowing genuine temptations and obstacles that must be refused and overcome. The reason the Lord even tolerates evil in the world is to produce a righteousness within us that not only withstands the assault of evil but also grows stronger and brighter in the midst of it.

Therefore, to deal with witchcraft, we must understand that the Lord's primary objective is not the removal of wickedness from society, but the transformation of our hearts to Christlikeness. As we become like Jesus—that is, loving our enemies, blessing those who curse us—Christ Himself literally and tangibly manifests Himself in our spirits. It is the transformed soul that dwells in the shelter of the Most High.

> *Father, help me to remember that Your plan has always been to conform me to Your likeness until I can love others—even my enemies—with perfect love. Help me to overcome every temptation and obstacle that crosses my path so that a pure heart and a steadfast spirit can be established within me. Thank You, Jesus, for Your work in me. Amen.*

MY SPIRITUAL PREPARATION FOR TODAY:

_____

_____

_____

GUARD YOUR TONGUE

*He who would love life and see good days, let him keep
his tongue from evil, and his lips from speaking deceit.*
—1 PETER 3:10

WE MUST COME to understand that each of our thoughts, and even our most intimate conversations with others, are actually prayers we are offering to the Father who sees all things continually and in secret. Our words about one another, as well as our words to one another, should carry with them the same sense of reverence as when we speak with God. For He is, indeed, listening.

The closer we truly draw to God, the more guilt we shall feel for our unclean words. When the Holy Spirit was revealed at Pentecost, He appeared as flaming tongues of fire. Certain segments of Christianity have made speaking in "other tongues" a sign of the infilling of the Holy Spirit. For us, the issue shall not be speaking in *foreign* tongues, but *flaming* tongues—tongues that have been purified by the fire of God, cleansed of fault-finding and criticisms.

> *Father, come now and touch me with Your tongues
> of fire and burn away any ungodliness found on my
> lips. May my words offer support and love to those I
> encounter today. May they be a shield of protection
> to those under duress from the enemy. Amen.*

MY SPIRITUAL PREPARATION FOR TODAY:

_____

_____

_____

BLESSING BREAKS CURSES

Bless those who persecute you; bless, and do not curse.
—ROMANS 12:14

How do we break the effect of curses and confusion that block our vision? We bless those who curse us. Even if we do not know specifically who is directing a curse toward us, we pray a blessing on them. In other words, we ask God to bless them with the same blessing we have experienced in our repentance and coming to Christ. We bless and curse not.

This is vital. Too many Christians become bitter and angry in the conflict. If we descend into hatefulness, we have already lost the battle against witchcraft. We must cooperate with God in turning what was meant for evil into a greater good within us. This is why we bless those who would curse us. It is not only for their sakes, but also to preserve our own soul from its natural response toward hatred.

> *Heavenly Father, You know the battle that is coming against me. I pray that You would pour out Your redemptive blessings—those very blessings that shatter darkness with light, that overcome evil with good, that bring hope to the hopeless and life to the dead. And I ask these things, heavenly Father, so that You might fulfill the redemptive purposes You revealed in Your Son, Jesus Christ, and satisfy the longing of Your heart. Amen.*

MY SPIRITUAL PREPARATION FOR TODAY:

_____

_____

_____

CASTING DOWN THE ACCUSER

And they loved not their lives unto the death.
—REVELATION 12:11

To LOVE NOT our life, even unto death, we cannot love our soul life more than our spirit life. We must maintain our love and faith, even when we face betrayal or injustice. We cannot overcome Satan and simultaneously harbor self-pity and sympathy for that which needs to be crucified within us. Our victory is consummated by our willingness to go even to death rather than betray our convictions of truth and love. The accuser must be cast down first in our minds. The kingdom of God and the authority of His Christ will be seen in a people who are terminally committed to love-motivated prayer.

> *Lord, let me be counted among those who are terminally committed to prayer motivated by Your great love. Teach me to love my spirit life more than my soul life so that I can overcome Satan and render him powerless. In Your mighty name, amen.*

MY SPIRITUAL PREPARATION FOR TODAY:

THE MANTLE OF PRAISE

Enter into His gates with thanksgiving, and into His courts with praise; be thankful to Him, and bless His name.
—PSALM 100:4

HOW DO WE *throw off the power of debilitation and oppression?* We put on the mantle of praise for the spirit of heaviness. The church is, by biblical definition, the house of the Lord, the temple of God. The purpose of the temple was not to "house" God, for even Heaven cannot contain Him. The temple was created to offer worship to the Almighty and to provide a place of access for us in God's habitation.

Thus, the Holy Spirit unites us so that we can provide a living temple where we offer continual worship to God. The battle against us seeks to keep us from that purpose.

If you are under an assault of witchcraft, begin to listen to praise music in your home or car. Sing along with it, letting your heart reach to the Lord. Build a buffer of worship around your soul. Become thankful for all that God has given you.

> *Thank You, Lord Jesus, for saving me, for delivering me from evil, and for the many times You answered my prayers and provided for me. Thank You for all the spiritual blessings You have won for me! Now, in the name of Jesus, I break the power of oppression as I worship Your holy name. Amen.*

MY SPIRITUAL PREPARATION FOR TODAY:

_____

_____

_____

WHAT WE AGREE UPON

Blessed is the man who walks not in the counsel of the ungodly, nor stands in the path of sinners, nor sits in the seat of scoffers.
—PSALM 1:1

WHATEVER A SOCIETY agrees upon and establishes through consent, compromise, and constant use will ultimately define reality to them. The Lord Himself said that whatever mankind imagined, it had the potential to accomplish. (See Genesis 11:6.)

Many scoffed when dreamers envisioned themselves standing on the moon. Many scorned the concept that voices and images could be transmitted around the world through invisible frequencies. Many ridiculed the idea that weapons would become powerful enough to destroy all life on earth. Yet today these things are part of our world because of man's power to establish reality. If a man's mind can imagine it and he can get others to believe in it, their spirits can accomplish it. And with few exceptions, nothing will be impossible, even for as small a group as two or three, once they believe a thing can happen. Understanding this precept is very important as we come into agreement with the principles and standards of the kingdom of God.

> *O Lord, infuse my human imagination with Your supernatural imagination so that I might know what it means to dream the impossible with You. Let my earthly reality give way to Your heavenly reality until I become one of Your world-changers. Amen!*

MY SPIRITUAL PREPARATION FOR TODAY:

_____

_____

Day 128

How to Overcome Fear

*Have not I commanded you? Be strong and
courageous. Do not be afraid or dismayed, for the
Lord your God is with you wherever you go.*
—Joshua 1:9

How do we overcome fear? God has not given us a spirit of fear, but of power, love, and a sound or disciplined mind (2 Tim. 1:7). Satan is a liar and the father of lies. The devil cannot tell the truth. No matter what Satan tells you, it is not the truth but a perversion of truth.

Jesus also said that Satan is a murderer. Whenever we believe the devil instead of God, the quality of our life proportionally declines; something in us dies, and it dies because we believed a lie. Therefore we must stop listening to Satan and simply do what the Lord tells us to do. The fears that bind us are often the result of the wavering, unresolved condition of our will. Once we decide to truly follow Christ, the bondage of fear can be overcome.

Lord God, forgive me for my fears. I confess that I have been seeking to save my life when You, in fact, have called me to lose it for Your sake. By the power of Your Spirit I renounce fear. God has not given me a spirit of fear! Father, I submit to the vision and courage of Your Son, Jesus, that I might live in accordance with Your will no matter what the cost. In Jesus's name, amen.

My spiritual preparation for today:

_____

_____

_____

Strength for the Battle

THE MEASURE OF YOUR LOVE

Let all that you do be done with love.
—1 CORINTHIANS 16:14

HOW OFTEN WE have heard people say, "I loved once, but I was hurt." Or, "I was committed to Christian service, but they used me." When someone withdraws his commitment to a relationship, he is withdrawing his love. It is not one's commitment that grows cold; it is their love. It may not seem like they have become cold—they may still attend church, sing, and look "Christian"—but inside they have become hard and separated from others. They have withdrawn from love. Because their commitment is shallow, they will be easily offended. Allow me to be perfectly clear: there is no such thing as love without commitment. *The measure of one's love is found in the depth of his or her commitment to others.*

> *Dear Lord, may I take the time today to renew my commitment to love others. I purpose today that I will not be a stumbling block by allowing my love to grow cold. Help me to forgive people for the hurts I've experienced in the past, and reignite a spark of passion in my heart to see others around me come to know You in new and deeper ways. Amen.*

MY SPIRITUAL PREPARATION FOR TODAY:

_____

_____

_____

_____

_____

ONENESS WITH GOD AND OTHERS

I in them and You in Me, that they may be perfect in unity.
—JOHN 17:23

THE MOST IMPORTANT goal in our lives is to walk in oneness with God Himself. Whether we discuss the attributes of humility, love, faith, worship, etc., the ultimate expression of each of these virtues is to functionalize our oneness with God.

Yet consequential to our oneness with the Lord is our growing oneness with others. That is to say, our unity with Christ also serves as our source of unity with one another, whether those relationships are with other Christians, or in marriage and family relationships, or even with our neighbors and friends. If we apply the standards set by Christ, they will lead us into some measure of unity with others, especially with Christians.

> *Jesus, I long for the perfect unity that You spoke of, and I am saddened when it is not present in the world around me. Help me to become a source of unity in my sphere of influence, applying the standards You set with a heart of love and compassion for all. Amen.*

MY SPIRITUAL PREPARATION FOR TODAY:

_____

_____

_____

_____

_____

_____

AGREEMENT WITH GOD

*So that now the manifold wisdom of God might be
made known by the church to the principalities and
powers in the heavenly places, according to the eternal
purpose which He completed in Christ Jesus our Lord.*
—EPHESIANS 3:10–11

WHEN IT COMES to angelic and demonic warfare, the battle
rests not in physical weaponry but in the *power of agreement* between mankind and the spirit realm. When the church
on earth is aggressive in its agreement with the will and Word
of God, then the presence of God increases in the spiritual
realm, proportionally displacing the influence of hell on earth.
Shortly thereafter, manifesting in the world of men, we see
revivals, healings, and miracles. But when the church is passive,
indifferent, or carnal, the powers of hell increase their rule over
the affairs of men: marriages break up, crime increases, and
wantonness becomes unbridled. We must see that our prayers,
attitudes, and agreement with God are an integral part of establishing the reality of the kingdom of God on earth!

> *Dear Lord, I come into agreement with Your will
> now, today, so that Your presence in the spiritual
> realm keeps increasing until hell has been displaced!
> Hallelujah! The Lord God Almighty reigns! Worthy
> is the Lamb! Amen!*

MY SPIRITUAL PREPARATION FOR TODAY:

CULTURAL TRANSFORMATION

*Brothers, do not be children in your thinking; rather
be infants in evil, but in your thinking be mature.*
—1 CORINTHIANS 14:20

PAUL TOLD US to "be eager to keep the unity of the Spirit...
until we all come into the unity of the faith and of the
knowledge of the Son of God, into a complete man, to the measure of the stature of the fullness of Christ" (Eph. 4:3, 13).

Note that verse 13 says: "Until we all...[become] a complete
man." The plural becomes singular when the goal is conformity
to Christ! When true Christ-centered unity is manifest, the
Father adds His endorsement: genuine miracles, transforming
power, and effective evangelism. Out of unity in the body of
Christ comes cultural transformation, the end of which is "that
the world may believe" (John 17:21).

> *Father, I am hungry to see Your genuine miracles
> and Your transforming power at work in the world
> today. Come into my church, I pray, and remove
> any obstacles to true Christ-centered unity that
> have festered there so that we may begin operating
> in all the fullness that Jesus paid for on the cross. If
> there is anything in me that has contributed to a
> lack of unity, take it from me now and replace it
> with Your Spirit. In Jesus's name, amen.*

MY SPIRITUAL PREPARATION FOR TODAY:

_____

_____

_____

The Sword of the Spirit

For the word of God is alive, and active, and sharper
than any two-edged sword, piercing even to the division
of soul and spirit, of joints and marrow, and able
to judge the thoughts and intents of the heart.
—Hebrews 4:12

The weapon God has given us to combat the lies of the enemy is the Word of God, which the Scriptures refer to as the "sword of the Spirit" (Eph. 6:17). Jesus said His words "are spirit and are life" (John 6:63), which is to say that the substance or meaning in Christ's words represents an actual reality: the living Spirit of the kingdom of God.

This point is essential: the singular weapon God has given the church is His Spirit-empowered Word. The living Word of the Spirit is the truth. To be successful in battle, we must know the Word of God.

> *Heavenly Father, put a burning in my heart for more of Your living Word. Make me an eager student of Scripture with a ravenous appetite for Your truths. Take Your living Word and infuse it deep within every strand of my DNA until it becomes the very breath of life to me.*

My spiritual preparation for today:

_____

_____

_____

_____

_____

THE UNITY OF THE GODHEAD

*I have given them the glory which You gave Me, that
they may be one even as We are one: I in them and
You in Me, that they may be perfect in unity.*
—JOHN 17:22–23

IF WE WILL sincerely pursue walking in the image of God,
remember: though He is three persons, it is written, "The
Lord our God is one Lord" (Mark 12:29). This model of three
persons, each working in divine and seamless symmetry, is the
image in the mind of God for man.

You see, the created pattern of "in the image of God" was
not only to reflect the reasoning and emotional qualities of
God, but in particular the *unity* of the Godhead. Even the
phrase "Let *us* make" speaks of the plurality within the singu-
larity of the Godhead.

Likewise the Lord desired to make man as an individual, singular, and yet in functionality, plural: "male and female" (Gen.
1:27). The man named the woman "Eve." God, however, called
them both "Mankind," for He saw the two as one (Gen. 5:2).
Thus, when we consider the outworking of the eternal idea—
that is, mankind in God's image—its fulfillment manifests
most perfectly in the Christ-centered unity of God's people.

> *Father God, how wonderful it is that I am created in
> Your image. I pray now for a harvest of Your inde-
> scribable triune presence that would manifest in all
> aspects of unity in the body of Christ. Amen.*

MY SPIRITUAL PREPARATION FOR TODAY:

_____

_____

WORSHIP IS WARFARE

Worship Him who made heaven and earth.
—REVELATION 14:7

IN THE LAST great battle before Jesus returns, the outcome of every man's life shall be weighed upon a scale of worship: In the midst of warfare and battles to whom will we bow, God or Satan?

The essence of this battle is the central issue in our warfare today. Will we faithfully worship God during satanic assault and temptation? True worship must emerge now in the context of our daily lives, for no man will worship through the great battles of tomorrow who complains in the mere skirmishes of today.

Without true worship of God there can be no victory in warfare. For what we bleed when we are wounded by satanic assault or difficult circumstances is the true measure of our worship. You see, what comes out of our hearts during times of pressure is in us, but hidden during times of ease. If you are a true worshipper, your spirit will exude worship to God no matter what battle you are fighting. In warfare, worship creates a wall of fire around the soul.

> *Father, today I confess that Jesus Christ is Lord in all that I do. I will proclaim His goodness from whatever "rooftop" I find myself on today. Give me courage not to shrink for fear of man. Make me bold today, Holy Spirit!*

MY SPIRITUAL PREPARATION FOR TODAY:

_____

_____

_____

CHOOSE LOVE

But the greatest of these is love.
—1 CORINTHIANS 13:13

ACCORDING TO GOD'S Word, when dealing with others, love is your only choice. What do I mean by love? I mean gentle, affectionate, sensitive, open, persistent love. God will be tough when He needs to be, and we will be firm when He tells us to be, but beneath our firmness must be an underground river of love waiting to spring into action.

By *love* I mean a compassion that is empowered by faith and prayer to see God's best come forth in the people I love. When I have love for someone, I have predetermined that I am going to stand with them, regardless of what they are going through. I am committed.

We each need people who love us, who are committed to us in spite of our imperfections. The fullness of Christ will not come without Christians standing with each other in love, until we care for each other, even as Christ has committed Himself to us.

> *Father, I humbly desire to love others the way that You have loved me. Help me to see others the way You see them, to feel the love for them that is in Your heart. Amen.*

MY SPIRITUAL PREPARATION FOR TODAY:

_____

_____

_____

_____

_____

THE MEASURE OF CHRIST'S LOVE

This is how we know the spirit of truth and the spirit of error. Beloved, let us love one another, for love is of God, and everyone who loves is born of God and knows God. Anyone who does not love does not know God, for God is love.
—1 JOHN 4:6–8

WE DISCERN THE spirit of truth from the spirit of error—or more specifically, the Spirit of Christ from the spirit of antichrist—by the measure of Christ's love operating in an individual or church. *An individual or church that thinks God is pleased with them, yet they do not walk in love, may actually be serving the spirit of antichrist.* Christians are to be known by their love, not merely their theology. (See John 13:35.)

Let us not defend those thoughts or attitudes that are "anti" Christ; rather, let us expose them as sin and see them defeated. if we can discern the difference between the loving voice of Christ and the arrogant rebellion of antichrist, we can take a major step toward seeing our lives conformed to our Savior.

> *Dear Jesus, give me holy discernment to recognize Your voice of love in the midst of the rebellious voices. I desire for my thoughts to conform to Your thoughts. Praise Your holy name! Amen.*

MY SPIRITUAL PREPARATION FOR TODAY:

_____

_____

_____

_____

_____

BE AGGRESSIVELY CALM

*Keep your heart with all diligence, for
out of it are the issues of life.*
—PROVERBS 4:23

SOLOMON WROTE, "BETTER is a full hand of quietness than handfuls of toil and chasing the wind" (Eccles. 4:6). There is too much labor and toil in our minds, too much striving and chasing the wind. If we want discernment, we must become aggressively calm. This is not a passive state of mind but an expectant, focused waiting upon God. Discernment comes from our sensitivity to Christ in the realm of the spirit. It comes as we allow love to be our motivation and secure the peace of Christ in our hearts. Through a life so prepared by God, the gift of discernment is revealed.

> *Lord, I am determined to be intentional about quieting my mind, heart, and spirit so that I can hear from You. As I tune out the distractions and stressful thoughts that can clutter my thinking, I will wait in the calmness for Your peace and direction. Amen.*

MY SPIRITUAL PREPARATION FOR TODAY:

_____

_____

_____

_____

_____

_____

BLESSING OR WRATH

*The curse of the LORD is on the house of the wicked,
but He blesses the habitation of the just.*
—PROVERBS 3:33

THERE IS A place in the expanse of God's omniscience where, to facilitate His plan to make man in His image, He allows us freedom of choice. If we obey Him, our lives move forward along the stream of His blessing. Here, He orchestrates all things to work for our good. Or, if we turn away from Him, we eventually position ourselves under the weight of His judgment. As such, we leave ourselves indefensible against evil. The Bible describes our freedom as the choice between God's blessing or His curse, and every soul has this choice. If we walk in obedience, we actually become a blessing. However, if we rebel against Him, our existence is under His wrath and our lives are accursed. An individual might be rich and famous but inwardly accursed and wretched, or one could be materially poor but inwardly blessed and full of life's truest joys. God's blessings are manifested in the quality of our lives, not the quality of our possessions.

Father, please come and put a governor on my heart in the power of Your Spirit that will give loud and clear warning should I begin to fall into the selfish ambition that leads to a rebellious heart. May I always make choices that position me to inherit Your blessing rather than Your wrath. I ask this in Jesus's name, amen.

MY SPIRITUAL PREPARATION FOR TODAY:

THE GOD OF THE LIVING

He is not the God of the dead, but of the living.
—MARK 12:27

THERE ARE MANY ways the antichrist spirit seeks to display itself as being God: the New Age movement, communism, etc. But the unique way it masquerades in the church as God is this: there is a natural, religious reverence men have toward death. Antichrist uses this phenomenon by conditioning congregations to accept the solemnity of death as though it were true reverence of God. The Almighty, however, is not the God of the dead but of the living, and true reverence is that which is accompanied by awe, joy, and thanksgiving.

When we better understand the antichrist spirit, we can war successfully against it through intercession, which discerns and binds this spirit of antichrist, releasing the church and allowing godly desires to prevail.

> *Heavenly Father, let me never forget who my living Savior is and that I too live because He lives. Help me to represent Jesus well in the world today, shedding His love and forgiveness everywhere I go like sweet perfume from Heaven. Amen.*

MY SPIRITUAL PREPARATION FOR TODAY:

_____

_____

_____

_____

_____

The Source of All Power

"For in Him we live and move and have our being." As some of your own poets have said, "We are His offspring."
—Acts 17:28

In the truest sense there is no power in the universe except that which comes from God. God is the sole Creator; He is the prime mover of all creation. John tells us that all things came into being through Him and apart from Him nothing exists. Hebrews tells us that, even now, the Lord is "upholding and maintaining and guiding and propelling the universe by His mighty word of power" (Heb. 1:3, AMPC).

Every moment of every day, in every aspect of our lives, we are governed by the interconnected, congruous expressions of God's power. As independent as we think we are, every breath, each thought, and every movement we make has its existence in the continuum of God's energy. There is nothing and no one hidden from His sight.

> *Father, let me press into Your Word today, remembering that You are the very source of my existence and You are the source of all power. Help me to remember my dependence upon You and that Your strength is made perfect in my weakness. Amen!*

My spiritual preparation for today:

_____

_____

_____

_____

BE A BOND SERVANT

For you have one Teacher, the Christ.
—MATTHEW 23:10

THE PENETRATION OF the antichrist spirit into typical Christian thinking is so deep that its deceptions are preached from pulpits and accepted in the pews. Therefore you must persevere for the sake of Christ in your community.

Let your faith continually increase while your fleshly ambitions proportionally decrease. Personal ambition is the motive of the antichrist; it is the name of the stronghold that has made us divided. You must approach others in the spirit of servanthood, not with the motive of fulfilling selfish ambition. If you are called to a leadership role, the others will recognize that call by your meekness and good fruit. Your ministry will come naturally, without self-promotion. In truth, God is not raising up leaders; He is training bond servants, men and women who will pray together for Christ's leading.

> *Lord, take me to Your Word and remind me afresh what servanthood looks like in Your kingdom. Let the meekness and humility of Jesus be manifested in my life. In the mighty name of Jesus, amen.*

MY SPIRITUAL PREPARATION FOR TODAY:

_____

_____

_____

_____

_____

JESUS CHRIST IS IN YOU

Examine yourselves, seeing whether you are in the faith; test yourselves. Do you not know this that Jesus Christ is in you?—unless indeed you are disqualified.
—2 CORINTHIANS 13:5

PAUL TAKES ALL of Christianity and sums up its entire body of truth into one irreplaceable reality: "Jesus Christ is in you." This reality is the one needful thing that Jesus said was necessary. We might be misinformed about the timing of the rapture or misguided in our administration of church government, but Paul says a true Christian is one who has accepted the living reality of Christ into their hearts!

Do you see this? We are saved, not because we said a prayer at an altar; we are saved because when we prayed, the Spirit of Jesus Christ actually entered our life! When He promises, "I will never leave you, nor forsake you" (Heb. 13:5), He means He is with us forever. The devil knows we are Christians not because we carry a Bible but because we actually carry Christ; Christ's presence is a flame of eternal life within us.

> *Precious Jesus, thank You for the privilege of bringing You, the Light of the World, with me everywhere. Remind me again today that nothing can snuff Your light out, nothing! Give me wisdom and vision so that I might not deviate from this most worthy of all goals. Amen.*

MY SPIRITUAL PREPARATION FOR TODAY:

_____

_____

_____

Seeing Clearly Is the Goal

First take the plank out of your own eye, and then you will
see clearly to take the speck out of your brother's eye.
—MATTHEW 7:5

THE EMPHASIS IN Jesus's command to "judge not" (Matt. 7:1) is summarized in His concluding remark in Matthew 7:5. *The way we help is not by judging but by seeing clearly.* And we do not see clearly until we have been through deep and thorough repentance, until the instinct to judge after the flesh is uprooted.

We have seen that Jesus paralleled speaking to people about their sins with taking specks out of their eyes. The eye is the most tender, most sensitive part of the human body. How do you take a speck out of someone's eye? *Very carefully!* First, you must win their trust. This means consistently demonstrating an attitude that does not judge, one that will not instinctively condemn. To help others, we must see clearly.

> *King Jesus, let me reflect Your humility today. Help me to first examine my own heart before I look at others. Let me remove the sin in my own life so that I might see clearly. Help me to remember that You have warned that You will judge me if I judge others. Amen.*

MY SPIRITUAL PREPARATION FOR TODAY:

_____

_____

_____

_____

_____

REDEMPTIVE VISION OF OTHERS

*They overcame him by the blood of the Lamb
and by the word of their testimony.*
—REVELATION 12:11

THE "WORD OF their testimony" includes testifying to others about the works of God, but it is also much more. "The testimony of Jesus," Scripture says, "is the spirit of prophecy" (Rev. 19:10). In other words, to truly overcome the voice of accusation we must live and think prophetically. We are to view each fellow disciple in Christ's church not according to their fleshly weaknesses but according to the redemptive vision granted us by God's transforming grace. We overcome the accuser by maintaining faith for each other, even when our brother or sister stumbles or falls. The word of our testimony is that God is good. He is faithful, and He will fulfill what He has promised concerning us.

> *Give me courage to never shrink from giving testimony for fear of what others may think. Let me trust instead in Your great power that is present in testimony so that I might live and think prophetically to the detriment of evil so that Your glory may be known in all the earth. Amen.*

MY SPIRITUAL PREPARATION FOR TODAY:

DAY 146

HE IS IMMANUEL

I am with you always, even to the end of the age.
—MATTHEW 28:20

IT IS CHRIST dwelling in us that produces fruit, works deliverance, and manifests power through us. Our living union with Him makes us His temple; our connectedness to Him enlivens us as His body.

Paul wrote, "Christ...lives in me" (Gal. 2:20). The Son of God is not a mere doctrine; He is Immanuel, "God with us." Eternal life comes from knowing God "and Jesus Christ, whom [God has] sent" (John 17:3).

So while there are many important doctrines, all of which are worthy of discussion, our single most important doctrine is that Christ is living within us—speaking, loving, healing, and guiding those born of His Spirit. When someone postures himself as a "keeper of the true faith," yet he rejects the reality of Jesus Christ living within us, that person reveals that he is the one walking in deception.

Jesus, I thank You that You have promised to always be with me. Let Your manifest presence season my words like salt today so that I may know how to answer everyone. Amen.

MY SPIRITUAL PREPARATION FOR TODAY:

_____

_____

_____

_____

_____

THE BATTLE HAS EXPANDED

*Then the serpent spewed water out of his mouth
like a flood after the woman, that he might cause
her [the church] to be carried away by the flood.*
—REVELATION 12:15

THE ACCESS THE devil has to the souls in our world has increased through the mass communications media and literature. John wrote of this period in time in Revelation 12:15.

Water, in this context, symbolizes "words." In our world there exists a flood of *words* and *visual images* coming out of the mouth of Satan. Our society, through technological advances, has made sins of the mind and heart more accessible. More than ever before, the carnal mind, with its openness to this satanic flood of filth and rebellion, is being structured into a powerful stronghold for the devil.

Therefore we must discern exactly where the satanic inroads are in our own lives and cut them off. We cannot worship God Sunday morning and then tolerate Jezebel through immoral entertainment in a movie Sunday night. For it is in the inner sanctuary of our soul life where tolerance to Jezebel begins. It is here, within us, where tolerance must end.

> *Dear Jesus, send Your Spirit into those places in the inner sanctuary of my soul and root out anything that gives shelter to the enemy. Let my love of anything carnal be displaced by all things beautiful and lovely that come only from You. Amen.*

MY SPIRITUAL PREPARATION FOR TODAY:

_____

_____

DAY 148

CHRIST IN US

If anyone loves Me, he will keep My word. My Father will love him, and We will come to him, and make Our home with him.
—JOHN 14:23

IN AN ERA of great confusion we must see truth as a person: Jesus Christ. Everything we need to know about God, Heaven, hell, salvation, sin, and redemption is centered in Him. We must also apply our hearts in humility and focused faith to become like Him, even as John taught, "Whoever says he remains in Him ought to walk as He walked" (1 John 2:6).

Eternal life does not come from having a religion *about* Christ but from actually *knowing Him* (John 17:3). He has purchased our forgiveness, our healing, and our well-being. As our Redeemer, He works all things for our good. As our King, He grants us His authority and sends us as His ambassadors. He calls us His body, underscoring His oneness with us. If anyone tries to convince you that Christ does not dwell within His people, remind them of His Word in John 14:23.

> *Jesus, I declare today that You, the living Son of God, are indeed a person, the most magnificent person who has ever lived! Send me out as a worthy ambassador today that I would be the sweet aroma of Christ among those who are being saved and those who are perishing. Amen.*

MY SPIRITUAL PREPARATION FOR TODAY:

_____

_____

_____

THE POWER OF THE TONGUE

*The tongue is a fire, a world of evil. The tongue is among
the parts of the body, defiling the whole body, and setting
the course of nature on fire, and it is set on fire by hell.*
—JAMES 3:6

MUCH OF WHAT the Father supplies to the body of Christ is
furnished through our confession. This is not simply our
positive, premeditated confession expressed in prayer; it consists
of everything that comes out of our mouths. Indeed, God has so
structured life that our very words, whether they are spoken in
faith or unbelief, play a determinant role in shaping our future.

If we desire life and the blessing of love and good days, we
must keep our tongues from speaking evil. We must use our
words to support, love, and protect each other. If we do, we
will experience much growth and greater protection. However,
if we are finding fault, criticizing, and bearing tales, the voice
of the accuser is manifested, and we are judged for our idle and
evil words. God looks at what we have said and gives us reality
accordingly.

> *O God, put the sword of Your Spirit in my mouth
> and my mind so that I might resist the devil and
> speak Your truth into the situations I encounter.
> May my words encourage others to draw closer to
> You and dispel the darkness. In Jesus's name, amen.*

MY SPIRITUAL PREPARATION FOR TODAY:

_____

_____

_____

THE VOICE OF THE ACCUSER

*Woe is me! For I am undone because I am a man of unclean
lips, and I dwell in the midst of a people of unclean lips.
For my eyes have seen the King, the LORD of Hosts.*
—ISAIAH 6:5

WHILE WE FREELY admit we do not know all the ways in
which Satan accuses man before God, we do offer one
solution. Christ has positioned our spirits in Him before God's
throne. While our spirits connect us to God, our bodies and
souls are here on earth. We have wrongly assumed that our
whispers spoken in darkness remained hidden even from God.
Is it not written, "What you have said in the darkness will be
heard in the light" (Luke 12:3)? Scripture tells us, "He who
would love life and see good days, let him keep his tongue from
evil, and his lips from speaking deceit" (1 Pet. 3:10).

The fact is, our criticisms of one another are the voice of Satan
accusing the saints before God. We cannot tolerate faultfinding
and accusations. We must possess the very heart of God toward
our brethren. When we see a need, instead of becoming critical, we must cast down the accuser of the brethren and pray!

> *Woe is me, Lord! I have unclean lips. Forgive me
> for my criticisms and judgmental attitudes toward
> others. Make me aware of the power of my words,
> even those spoken in private. Help me to remember
> to bless others and not to curse or accuse them. In
> Your precious name I pray, amen.*

MY SPIRITUAL PREPARATION FOR TODAY:

_____

_____

WHEN BAD BECOMES GOOD

We know that all things work together for good to those who
love God, to those who are called according to His purpose.
—ROMANS 8:28

A LL OF US receive a portion of both good and evil in this
world. But for life to be good, God, who is the essence
of life, must reach into our experiences and redeem us from
our negative reactions. The channel through which the Lord
extends Himself, even into our past, is our love and worship
of Him.

The key for the fulfillment of Romans 8:28 is that we become
lovers of God in our spirits. Bad things become good for "those
who love God." When we are given to loving Him, all that we
have passed through in life is washed and redeemed in that
love. Bad becomes good by the power of God. Therefore it is
essential to both the salvation of our souls and our protection
in warfare that we be worshippers. The ship that safely carries
us through the storms of adversity is worship.

Father, I ask You to wash me afresh in Your love
and give me the courage to trust that You have been
and are working all things for my good. Let me see
the past in the light of Your love and trust You for
my future. Amen.

MY SPIRITUAL PREPARATION FOR TODAY:

_____

_____

_____

_____

THE DOORWAY OF UNREPENTANT SINS

*If we confess our sins, He is faithful and just to forgive
us our sins and cleanse us from all unrighteousness.*
—1 JOHN 1:9

TO FIND AN indictment against the church, it is important to note that the enemy must draw his accusations from
hell. If we have repented of our sins, no record of them or our
mistakes exists in Heaven. As it is written, "Who shall bring
a charge against God's elect? It is God who justifies" (Rom.
8:33). Even while the Lord will speak to us of our sin and need
of repentance, He is not condemning us. Rather, He is at the
Father's right hand interceding on our behalf.

Let us, therefore, expose the weapons of the enemy. The first
weapon used against us is our unrepentant sins. Our failure to
repent when the Holy Spirit desires to correct us opens the door
for the accuser to condemn us. The way to defeat the enemy in
this arena is to disarm him by sincerely repenting of the sin,
confessing it to someone trustworthy, and then looking again
to the atonement of Christ as the source of all our righteousness.

> *Dear Lord, I ask You to forgive me for those things
> that I have not been willing to admit are sinful in
> Your eyes. Teach me to be so sensitive to Your gentle
> conviction that I immediately repent and ask for Your
> forgiveness. Let me live so there is no hindrance to
> keep me from fulfilling Your call on my life. Amen.*

MY SPIRITUAL PREPARATION FOR TODAY:

_____

_____

_____

THE WAR OVER REALITY

As you have believed, so let it be done for you.
—MATTHEW 8:13

HOW DOES LIFE appear—to you? The dictionary defines *reality* as "that which is real; an actual thing, situation, or event." Such is reality in terms of objective analysis. But reality is not just objective: there is also a subjective or personal side to reality that is rooted in our feelings, attitudes, and beliefs. From this perspective life is done for us as we have believed (Matt. 8:13).

Created in the image of God, man was given limited, yet distinct, inherent powers. He was granted the power to imagine, as well as the faculty to define and then establish reality. And, operating within the boundaries preset by God, man does this, for better or worse, according to the free selection of his will. As we understand this, we see that the essence of spiritual warfare is in what shall define reality: the Word of God or the illusions of this present age.

> *O Father, open my eyes afresh today to the reality of Jesus Christ so that I might truly begin to believe. Give me an explosive revelation of the Eternal that will propel me from my place of complacency into a direct confrontation with Jesus that takes me deep into Your heart of grace. Let my reality be defined by the truth of Your Word and not the current thinking of the culture around me. I want to know You more! Amen.*

MY SPIRITUAL PREPARATION FOR TODAY:

_____

_____

DAY 154

SAFEGUARDING THE PROPHETIC

Your word is truth.
—JOHN 17:17

THE POWER RELEASED by a humble, accurate, new covenant prophet can be a revelation of the Lord Himself, causing people to fall on their faces in worship (1 Cor. 14:25). I have often been encouraged and guided by a prophetic word. Confirmed prophetic words, as Paul wrote Timothy, are spiritual weapons. They help us "fight a good fight" (1 Tim. 1:18).

Yet there are boundaries. Writing as "a wise master builder" (1 Cor. 3:10), Paul counseled, "Let two or three prophets speak, and let the others judge" (1 Cor. 14:29). The admonition to minister as "two or three" instead of as a singular individual is an important safeguard. First, it tells us that no matter how spiritual we consider ourselves, we do not see the whole picture; we need others. Jesus sent His disciples out in twos. He also spoke of the power that is released when two or three disciples gathered in His name. The Revelation of John tells us that the last great prophetic move will be heralded by two prophets (not one) speaking and ministering together (Rev. 11).

Father, I pray for discernment in the church regarding prophetic ministry. Give us Your definition of new covenant prophecy so that we might not be led astray but be encouraged, guided, and enriched by what You speak to us through the prophets You establish. Amen.

MY SPIRITUAL PREPARATION FOR TODAY:

_____

_____

WHAT JEZEBEL HATES

*Yes, all of you be submissive one to another and
clothe yourselves with humility, because "God resists
the proud, but gives grace to the humble."*
—1 PETER 5:5

JEZEBEL HATES REPENTANCE. Her worst fear is that the people will begin to mourn over their sins. Though this spirit will infiltrate the church, masking its desire for control with true Christian doctrines, it will hide from true repentance.

Jezebel hates humility. Jesus taught that greatness in the kingdom was measured in childlike honesty of heart. We must learn that spirituality is measured in meekness, not intellectual power.

Jezebel hates prayer. Intercessory prayer pries her fingers off the hearts and souls of men. It sets people free in the spirit. When you pray, it binds her.

Jezebel hates the prophets, for the prophets speak out against her. Yet more than her hatred for the prophetic ministry, she hates the words they speak. Her real enemy is the spoken Word of God.

Jezebel's ultimate hatred is against God Himself. She hates the holiness and purity of heart that come from God and surround those who serve in His courts.

> *Father, I submit to You and Your standard of righteousness. I ask for purity, meekness, and holiness of heart. I ask for the joy of a humble and submissive spirit and pull down the imaginations of ambition and pride. In Jesus's name, amen!*

MY SPIRITUAL PREPARATION FOR TODAY:

Let the Lord Confirm It

Let two or three prophets speak, and let the others judge.
—1 Corinthians 14:29

Are you a prophet? Instead of saying, "Thus sayeth the Lord," it would be wiser and probably truer to say, "I have a witness for you. Let the Lord confirm it." If you are being ministered to by a prophet and have any question about what is being said, give the Holy Spirit time to confirm His Word through one or two more people (unless you have an immediate confirmation in your spirit that the word is God's).

What if you believe you have a warning to issue? I'd suggest you speak it first privately to your peers, as well as to the church leaders where the warning applies. Let someone outside your local ministry team confirm it independently. Give God time to arrange a supernatural presentation of His will. The combination of words that have been confirmed supernaturally by prophetic leaders from different ministries is a powerful catalyst for faith.

Do not be afraid to let your witness be judged, and if you question a prophetic witness, don't be shy about humbly saying that you don't bear witness.

> *Father, I desire integrity in the body of Christ, particularly for prophetic ministry. Teach us how to steward well those gifts You have placed within us. We desire the fullness of Your supernatural revelation that our faith might rise in this hour. In Jesus's name, amen.*

My spiritual preparation for today:

_____

_____

_____

DON'T SETTLE FOR THE STATUS QUO

That He might present to Himself a glorious church,
not having spot, or wrinkle, or any such thing, but
that it should be holy and without blemish.
—EPHESIANS 5:27

WARFARE IN THE church today is centered upon the fact that the devil wants us to accept Christianity as it is—as though division, sin, and spiritual impotency were the ultimate reality God has provided for believers on earth. Satan wants us to *agree with and thereby reinforce* this deceptive view of the church.

There are many promises that are yet to be fulfilled concerning the people of God. These are holy and noble purposes that shall unfold in the last days. Therefore our agreement must be with *God's plan* for a holy, undivided, powerful church, for He is calling us to establish *His* kingdom, not the status quo!

> *Father, help me to realize the power of my prayers,*
> *my attitudes, and my agreement with You. They*
> *are key components in establishing the reality of*
> *Your kingdom on earth. Help me avoid the trap*
> *of accepting the status quo and thinking this is all*
> *there is to Christianity and the kingdom of God.*

MY SPIRITUAL PREPARATION FOR TODAY:

_____

_____

_____

_____

_____

TO THE VICTOR GOES THE NATION

The LORD your God is in your midst, a Mighty One, who will
save. He will rejoice over you with gladness, He will renew
you with His love, He will rejoice over you with singing.
—ZEPHANIAH 3:17

THERE IS A war, a very ancient war, between the spirit of
Elijah and the spirit of Jezebel. In this age-old battle Elijah
represents the interests of Heaven: the call to repentance and
the return to God. Jezebel, on the other hand, represents that
unique principality whose purpose is to hinder and defeat the
work of repentance. To understand the conflict between the
Elijah spirit and the spirit of Jezebel, we must understand these
two adversaries as they are seen in the Scriptures. Each is the
spiritual counterpart of the other. The war between Elijah and
Jezebel continues today. The chief warriors on either side are the
prophets of both foes; to the victor goes the soul of the nation.

> *Father, put a hedge of protection around me today*
> *that I would not give in to fear and discouragement*
> *in the face of whatever warfare the enemy tries to*
> *throw against me in the midst of this ancient Jezebel*
> *battle. In Your mighty name, amen.*

MY SPIRITUAL PREPARATION FOR TODAY:

_____

_____

_____

_____

_____

A NEW PROPHETIC ANOINTING

*Do not despise prophecies. Examine all
things. Firmly hold onto what is good.*
—1 THESSALONIANS 5:20–21

THE WITNESS OF the prophetic should always be measured against the truth of Scripture and the voice and motive of the Holy Spirit. The prophetic ministry is not a law unto itself but is presented as a humble, yet powerful, revelation of Christ—one that is accountable to church authority.

If you have felt manipulated or wounded by false prophetic words, whether concerning the Lord's return or an imminent disaster or a personal word you were given, I pray you will not lose faith or become cynical.

I ask you to forgive those in the prophetic movement who, in an attempt to serve the Lord, may have misrepresented the will and timing of God. Yes, there is a prophetic mess at times, but there are also blessings, as God's Word affirms. Let's pray for a new prophetic anointing to fall.

> *Heavenly Father, forgive us for failing to accurately represent Your will. I pray today for a new prophetic anointing to fall on the whole church. Teach us how to steward the powerful revelation of Jesus Christ with humility and accountability, to the glory of Your name. Amen.*

MY SPIRITUAL PREPARATION FOR TODAY:

_____

_____

_____

MORE THAN WHAT WE SEE NOW

*For now we see as through a glass, dimly, but
then, face to face. Now I know in part, but then
I shall know, even as I also am known.*
—1 CORINTHIANS 13:12

WHILE WE MUST work with the church as it is, we must ever realize that what we see in Christianity is not what the church will be like before Jesus returns. In fact, our call is to cooperate with God in the bringing forth of revival and the raising up of the body of Christ. Our quest is to serve the vision of the Lord until He presents to Himself the church in all her glory, holy and blameless (Eph. 5:27).

Before Jesus returns, the Father has promised His Son a bride without spot or wrinkle. She shall be a powerful witness of Christ Himself in the earth.

> *Father, give me spiritual eyes to see more than what I can see around me in the natural. Prepare my heart for Your purposes and plans for the last days so that I can be a powerful witness and part of the spotless bride awaiting Your return. Amen.*

MY SPIRITUAL PREPARATION FOR TODAY:

_____

_____

_____

_____

_____

_____

THE FATHER'S PLAN

For as the body is one and has many parts, and all the many parts of that one body are one body, so also is Christ.
—1 CORINTHIANS 12:12

THE FATHER'S PLAN to create man in "the image of God," as stated in His original purpose in Genesis 1:26–27, is through the indwelling of Christ in the church. When Jesus says we will be able to discern the true from the false by their fruit, He is speaking precisely of seeing the fruit of His living presence manifest through us. If we know Him, we will know those who say they represent Him by their fruits (Matt. 7:15–20). For He is the source of our fruitfulness.

> *O Father, source of all fruitfulness, take me and use me today to reveal the character, motivation, and spiritual gifts of Jesus Christ in order to see the fully functioning nature of Christ come to greater fruition in the church. Manifest Your living presence through me today so that others see in me the love and compassion of Jesus. Let me stand in that place of grace with You today. In Jesus's name, amen.*

MY SPIRITUAL PREPARATION FOR TODAY:

THE REALM OF FINAL VICTORY

I am He who searches the hearts and minds.
—REVELATION 2:23

YOU CANNOT DEFEAT the enemy simply with prayer. To topple Satan's empire we must be transformed into Christ's likeness. *We cannot be successful in the heavenly war if we are not victorious in the battlefield of our minds.* There is only one realm of final victory against the enemy: Christlikeness.

It is Jesus who searches our "hearts and minds." Our victory in every battle begins here. Consequently we cannot tolerate Jezebelian thinking in any area. Our concept of church must expand beyond buildings into a way of life we practice everywhere. Since we are the church, let us realize that we are still in the church when we are home. When we turn on television to an immoral program or view a website that is illicit, we are still in the church, tolerating the spirit of Jezebel. Our time spent in the worship service is necessary, but it is a very small part of our continuing church life. It is in our daily, routine living where the strongholds of Jezebel must be confronted and destroyed.

> *Holy Spirit, give me victory on the battlefield of the mind today so that I can stand as one whose inner purity reflects Your outward glory from the church to the world. Amen!*

MY SPIRITUAL PREPARATION FOR TODAY:

_____

_____

_____

_____

LOOK FOR THE REVELATION OF CHRIST

So he shepherded them according to the integrity of his heart and guided them by the skillfulness of his hands.
—PSALM 78:72

To THE DEGREE that all of us, different as we are, flow together in love, honor, and unity, to that measure Christ is revealed to the world through the church. Where there might be differences in the church, and these differences might cause division, our oneness in Christ showcases the life of His kingdom, which is a culture of harmony, power, and love.

Of course, no one is perfect or complete yet. We are looking to discern the treasure hidden in the field. A pastor or teacher may be imperfect in many ways. But his goal should be apparent: he is seeking daily to become more like Christ.

I am not saying theology or doctrinal matters are unimportant. God forbid! No, but there is something that transcends right knowledge, and that is a right heart. Paul said, "Follow me as I follow Christ" (1 Cor. 11:1).

> *Father, I pray for those in the church today. Give us the desire to showcase our unity in Christ by promoting Your culture of harmony, power, and love to the world around us. Amen.*

MY SPIRITUAL PREPARATION FOR TODAY:

_____

_____

_____

_____

_____

DAY 164

STAND ON THE WORD OF GOD, PART 1

Your word is a lamp to my feet and a light to my path.
—PSALM 119:105

IF YOU ARE in need of deliverance, or if you are being used in the ministry of deliverance, the following verses (continued on Day 165) will be helpful in establishing victory. It is not wise to engage in any kind of spiritual warfare without knowing these scriptures perfectly from memory.

"Do not have fellowship with the unfruitful works of darkness; instead, expose them" (Eph. 5:11). When you expose and confess your sins, they no longer are in darkness (secrecy). When light is turned on in a dark room, darkness becomes light. So also when you bring your sins out of darkness and expose them to light, they vanish in God's forgiveness; they become light.

"If we confess our sins, He is faithful and just to forgive us our sins and cleanse us from all unrighteousness" (1 John 1:9).

"Now thanks be to God who always causes us to triumph in Christ and through us reveals the fragrance of His knowledge in every place" (2 Cor. 2:14). There is victory, right here, right now, because Christ is in you.

> Today, Lord, I seek to know and memorize Your Word because it has the power to change my life and the lives of those around me. The devil's lies are easy to discern when held up against the truth of Scripture. Help me not only to memorize it but also do what it says. Amen.

MY SPIRITUAL PREPARATION FOR TODAY:

_____

_____

STAND ON THE WORD OF GOD, PART 2

For the word of God is alive, and active, and sharper
than any two-edged sword, piercing even to the division
of soul and spirit, of joints and marrow, and able
to judge the thoughts and intents of the heart.
—**HEBREWS 4:12**

THE FOLLOWING VERSES (continued from Day 164) are helpful in spiritual warfare and should be memorized.

"For God has not given us the spirit of fear, but of power, and love, and self-control" (2 Tim. 1:7). Don't fear Satan's threats. Remember, the devil is "a liar" and "there is no truth in him" (John 8:44).

"Through death He might destroy him who has the power of death, that is, the devil, and deliver those who through fear of death were throughout their lives subject to bondage" (Heb. 2:14–15). Use the name of Jesus and the Word of God to break the power of Satan's lies.

"We know that all things work together for good to those who love God, to those who are called according to His purpose" (Rom. 8:28). If God causes everything to work for good as you love Him, then ultimately nothing bad can ever happen to you.

Beautiful Savior, I pick up my authority, won on the cross, and with confidence and boldness in the One who saved me, I believe in Your Word and I know that it has the power to cause victory, breakthrough, deliverance, and healing in my life! Yes and amen!

MY SPIRITUAL PREPARATION FOR TODAY:

_____

_____

DAY 166

STAND ON THE WORD OF GOD, PART 3

*Therefore you must fix these words of mine
in your heart and in your soul.*
—DEUTERONOMY 11:18

THE FOLLOWING VERSES (continued from Day 165) are helpful in spiritual warfare and should be memorized.

"Look, I give you authority to trample on serpents and scorpions, and over all the power of the enemy. And nothing shall by any means hurt you" (Luke 10:19). Jesus has given us authority over all of Satan's power. We have His authority and His promise that nothing shall injure us!

"For this purpose the Son of God was revealed, that He might destroy the works of the devil" (1 John 3:8). You have been set free—not because you feel free, but because you have faith. Each time you speak your faith, you are *establishing* your freedom as a true reality. Your confidence is that while you are praying, the angelic hosts of God, which outnumber the devil by at least two to one, are united with you against evil. With Jesus you cannot fail! (See also Isaiah 42:13; 53; 54:11–17; Romans 10:8–9; Ephesians 6:18; James 4:7.)

Thank You, God, for giving us Your Word. Help me to commit more of it to memory so that I can use it effectively in warfare against the enemy. Amen.

MY SPIRITUAL PREPARATION FOR TODAY:

_____

_____

_____

_____

THE PERFECTION OF LOVE

For the anger of man does not work the righteousness of God.
—JAMES 1:20

THE GOSPELS REPEATEDLY reveal that the great majority of Christ's life was given in love for mankind. From healing the sick to driving out demons to laying down His life for men, His heart was compelled by love, even to His dying prayer: "Father, forgive them" (Luke 23:34). Jesus did not let His outrage minimize His capacity to love. He is the Good Shepherd. And even while people slandered Him, His attitude was always, "Whoever speaks a word against the Son of Man will be forgiven" (Matt. 12:32).

What we see in Jesus Christ is the perfection of love, not judgment. Actually, the perfection of love *is* the perfection of judgment. And while we might have brief moments of righteous anger, let us remember the Lord's admonition: let him who is without sin cast the first stone (John 8:7).

> *Dear Lord, work in me the perfection of Your love so that the judgment that is in my heart must give way to Your love as the Good Shepherd. Make me a little more like Jesus today. Thank You, Father. Amen.*

MY SPIRITUAL PREPARATION FOR TODAY:

_____

_____

_____

_____

_____

THE INFLUENCE OF BABYLON

And I heard a loud voice from heaven, saying, "Look!
The tabernacle of God is with men, and He will
dwell with them. They shall be His people, and God
Himself will be with them and be their God."
—REVELATION 21:3

YOU WILL REMEMBER it was Babylon that conquered the Hebrews and carried them off into captivity. There Daniel was raised up to sit with the Chaldean wise men and conjurers who counseled King Nebuchadnezzar. We see this spirit in the thinking of the Babylonian priests when they were required to know what only the Almighty knew. They said, "It is a rare thing that the king requires, and there is no one else who can tell it before the king, except the gods whose dwelling is not with flesh" (Dan. 2:11).

We can recognize the influence of Babylon in any people or church that offers lip service to a God far off, a deity whose dwelling place is not with men. In contrast, Jesus is our Immanuel, "God with us." The very essence of true Christianity is Christ in us, the hope of glory. You can discern the spirit of Babylon in a church that honors God in Heaven without having any relationship with Him on earth.

> *Father, forgive me for sometimes being one that honors*
> *You in Heaven without having any relationship with*
> *You on earth. Give me courage to fight the compro-*
> *mising spirit of Babylon lest I fall into captivity! Amen.*

MY SPIRITUAL PREPARATION FOR TODAY:

_____

_____

THE WINDOW OF SCRIPTURE

So then faith comes by hearing, and hearing by the word of God.
—ROMANS 10:17

THE MOST IMPORTANT revelation you can have when reading the Word, and especially the Gospels, is the realization that you're not just studying doctrine or rules; you are gazing upon God Himself. The Scriptures become a window through which you can actually see God. When I find myself face to face with the chaos of my fleshly nature, I do not hide my darkness from the Lord. Rather, I thrust myself, darkness and all, into the fire of His creative love and abilities. I know that what He will do in me is not unlike what He did with the pre-creation universe.

> *Let Your Word be my window into Your heart today, Lord. When the chaos of my fleshly nature threatens to draw me into darkness, take me and throw me in the fiery furnace of Your creative love as found in Scripture until I am made new again! Reveal to me afresh the wonderful salvation that is mine in Jesus Christ. Hallelujah and amen!*

MY SPIRITUAL PREPARATION FOR TODAY:

_____

_____

_____

_____

_____

_____

_____

DAY 170

CALLED OUT OF BABYLON

*"Come out of her, my people," lest you partake in
her sins, and lest you receive her plagues.*
—REVELATION 18:4

WHEN WE ARE called out of Babylon, it is a call into Christ-likeness. In this hour God is certainly calling the church to enter into meekness, moderation, and purity of heart. The Holy Spirit has been judging and cleansing the Babylonian strongholds from the church. Indeed, the sins of Babylon will soon be fulfilled by plagues, which even now are falling upon her. In His mercy God calls us out of this evil.

The spirit of Babylon is all around us, both in our society in general and in the Christian church in particular. Anytime we decide to coexist with the devil, it leaves us desolate and naked, suffering in unquenchable fire. This warning must be heard by each of us as individuals. In the sanctuary of our hearts we must decide we are not going to compromise with Babylon in any way.

> *Thank You, God, that in Your mercy You call us out of Babylon, out of evil. Come now and remove from me any pride, worldliness, and lust for pleasure that would draw me into that place of compromise that seeks to separate me from You. I hear Your call to Christlikeness in this hour! Make me meek and pure of heart, Lord of Heaven and earth. Amen.*

MY SPIRITUAL PREPARATION FOR TODAY:

_____

_____

_____

THE HUMAN SIDE OF JESUS

*For we do not have a High Priest who cannot
sympathize with our weaknesses, but One who was in
every sense tempted like we are, yet without sin.*
—HEBREWS 4:15

I NEED TO MAKE it clear that I do not see Christ as one without
anger. There are evil things in our world that are actually
"an abomination before God" (Luke 16:15), and Jesus abhorred
them. He was obviously grieved concerning the callousness,
pride, and lack of compassion in the Pharisees and scribes of
His day. (See Matthew 23.) He also reproved His disciples for
their jealousy and selfish ambition (Matt. 20:20–28). And He
rebuked the masses for their unbelief, complacency, and failure
to discern the times (Matt. 11:21; Luke 19:44). Worst of all would
be the anger Jesus felt toward someone who "misleads one of
these little ones who believe in Me" (Matt. 18:6).

If we desire to be like Christ, we must remember these attributes as well. Indeed, these passions, along with the times Jesus
wept (Luke 19:41; John 11:35), reveal a very human side to our
Lord. If we are alive to the heart of God, we will certainly have
times when we are outraged by sin in this world.

> *Lord, do not let my outrage minimize my capacity
> to love. Instead, let righteous anger stir in me a
> greater passion for Your great heart. Amen.*

MY SPIRITUAL PREPARATION FOR TODAY:

_____

_____

_____

THOSE WHO CONQUER

*Rejoice over her, O heaven and saints and apostles
and prophets, for God has avenged you against her.*
—REVELATION 18:20

As WE AGREE in spirit and character, in word and behavior,
with the Word of God concerning righteousness, God will
put in our mouths His judgments concerning evil. We are not
fighting flesh and blood but the powers of darkness that hold
people captive. "By the church" the manifold wisdom of God
is made known "to the principalities and powers in the heavenly places" (Eph. 3:10). Before Jesus returns, His church will
be brought up to His standard in all aspects. (See Ephesians
4:11–15.) And that includes becoming an army that hates wickedness and loves righteousness, an army that, as it follows Christ,
initiates spiritual warfare against the various gates of hell.

*Father, I enlist in Your army today, agreeing in
spirit and character, in word and behavior, with
Your Holy Word concerning all righteousness. May
the simplicity and purity of my life be instrumental
in the battle against the forces of evil, revealing Your
manifold wisdom to the principalities and powers in
heavenly places until Jesus returns. Amen.*

MY SPIRITUAL PREPARATION FOR TODAY:

_____

_____

_____

_____

_____

THE POWER OF REDEMPTION

Love your enemies, bless those who curse you...that
you may be sons of your Father who is in heaven. For
He makes His sun rise on the evil and on the good.
—MATTHEW 5:44–45

EXPERIENCING THE EFFECTS of witchcraft might not be a common occurrence, but the symptoms are as follows: Witchcraft will cause confusion. You'll lose track of your spiritual vision and feel mentally weakened, even physically clumsy. Witchcraft will also stimulate unreasonable fear and engender strife between you and others. Of course, there are natural sources for all these symptoms as well, but the ones I mentioned are what typically accompany witchcraft.

The main source for witchcraft is not what comes from non-Christians but what comes through the mouths of gossiping, negative church members.

If you have been a target of negativity or gossip, Jesus gave a clear path to victory in Matthew 5, instructing us to see it as an opportunity to become Christlike.

> *Father, I take all negativity and gossip that has been leveled against me and leave it at the foot of Your cross. Right now I lift up in love my enemies and those who persecute me. May they come to know the forgiveness that is theirs in Jesus Christ. Amen!*

MY SPIRITUAL PREPARATION FOR TODAY:

_____

_____

_____

KNOW JESUS

Your people will follow you in the day of your battle.
—PSALM 110:3

D O YOU HEAR the war cry our King is raising? It is the call to put away the idols of Babylon and approach the hour of our destiny with zeal and willing obedience to Jesus. Especially as we approach the end of this age, it is essential we understand that God's purpose is to conform us to the image of His Son. We are to grow up "in all aspects" of the Holy One, even into His likeness as Captain of the Hosts!

As you enter into the administration of the victory of Jesus Christ, what was once a walk filled with blindness and darkness will now become a walk of vision and light. Your words will declare God's purpose, and His purpose will empower your words. You will rejoice as you see the Spirit of God "judge your judgment" of Babylon.

> *Heavenly Father, we worship You! We declare that Your name shall be exalted in all the earth. Take me today and grow me up in all aspects of the Holy One so that I walk in vision and light, declaring Your purposes and rejoicing in Your presence. Hallelujah! Amen!*

MY SPIRITUAL PREPARATION FOR TODAY:

A BETTER WAY

He who believes in Me will do the works that I do also.
—JOHN 14:12

As CHRISTIANS, WE must guard against prejudging all Muslims, for many people turned to Islam as a reaction to the sinfulness of the West. In a real way they were seeking God, but the church failed them. In this present atmosphere, however, they now doubt the choice they made to follow Islam. Therefore we must reveal Christ and the love He has for all people if we hope to win Muslims.

We must forgive and pray for Muslims, that the Lord of the harvest would send laborers into the Muslim world and that Jesus would be revealed to them, including the most radical. The radical Islamist will only be won by the radical Christ follower. We must show them a better way.

Father, remove any fear that would keep me from Your heart of love for all people, including Muslims. Help me to share Jesus with others even when their actions and beliefs frighten me. Make me bold for the gospel. In Jesus's name, amen.

MY SPIRITUAL PREPARATION FOR TODAY:

_____

_____

_____

_____

_____

_____

DAY 176

DISCERNING THE NATURE OF THE ENEMY

*Therefore God highly exalted Him and gave Him
the name which is above every name, that at the
name of Jesus every knee should bow, of those in
heaven and on earth and under the earth.*
—PHILIPPIANS 2:9–10

IN THE REALM of the spirit the name of an entity always cor-
responds to its nature. You will notice that there are many
names given to the Lord in Scripture. Yet each revealed name
was actually a deeper revelation of His nature. (See Genesis
22:14; Exodus 3:14.) Similarly the names of the Lord's angels are
also self-descriptive.

This principle of consistency between the name and nature
of spiritual beings holds true in discerning the activity and
purpose of evil spirits. To defeat the rulers of darkness we must
know their nature—what to expect, what their tactics are, and
how they apply those tactics against our weaknesses.

*Glorious Lord, You are the Almighty, our advocate,
the Alpha and Omega, the author and finisher of our
faith, the beloved Son, the bread of life, the branch,
the desire of the nations, the everlasting Father, the
faithful witness, the first and last, and so much more.
All honor and glory are Yours, O Lord of all!*

MY SPIRITUAL PREPARATION FOR TODAY:

_____

_____

_____

_____

BORN OF THE LIGHT

I have come as a light into the world, that whoever
believes in Me should not remain in darkness.
—JOHN 12:46

MANY CHRISTIANS DEBATE whether the devil is on the earth or in hell; can he dwell in Christians or only in the world? The fact is, the devil is in darkness. Wherever there is spiritual darkness, there the devil will be. It is vital to recognize that this darkness to which Satan has been banished is not limited to areas outside of humanity. Unlike those who do not know Jesus, however, we have been delivered out of the domain or "authority" of darkness. We are not trapped in darkness if we have been born of light. But if we tolerate darkness through tolerance of sin, we leave ourselves vulnerable for satanic assault. For wherever there is willful disobedience to the Word of God, there is spiritual darkness and the potential for demonic activity.

> *Jesus, search every corner of my heart and clean out the hidden things that lurk in the dark. Shine Your light of love and forgiveness in every part of my being so that I give no place to the enemy. In Your name, amen.*

MY SPIRITUAL PREPARATION FOR TODAY:

_____

_____

_____

_____

_____

SEARCH YOUR HEART

Search me, O God, and know my heart; try me, and know my concerns, and see if there is any rebellious way in me, and lead me in the ancient way.
—PSALM 139:23–24

SPIRITUAL DISCERNMENT IS the grace to see into the unseen. It is a gift of the Spirit to perceive the realm of the spirit. Its purpose is to understand the nature of that which is veiled. However, the first veil that must be removed is the veil over our own hearts. For the capacity to see into that which is in another's heart comes from Christ revealing that which is in our own hearts. Before He reveals the sin of another, Jesus demands we grasp our own deep need of His mercy. Thus, out of the grace that we have received, we can compassionately minister grace to others. We will know thoroughly that the true gift of discernment is not a faculty of our minds.

> *Father, forgive me for those times I have not been willing to examine my own heart with honesty and humility. Before I discern anything in someone else's life, may I always seek You first for those things that are not pleasing in my own life and confess them to make my heart right with You. In the name of Your Son, Jesus, I pray, amen.*

MY SPIRITUAL PREPARATION FOR TODAY:

_____

_____

_____

_____

BE ASSURED IN CHRIST

*I saw Satan as lightning fall from heaven. Look, I
give you authority to trample on serpents and
scorpions, and over all the power of the enemy.
And nothing shall by any means hurt you.*
—LUKE 10:18–19

A S WE EMBRACE God's eternal plan, which is to make us
in the image of Christ, let us remember that no weapon
formed against us shall prosper, and every tongue that accuses
us in judgment we will condemn (Isa. 54:17). As we capture
every thought unto the obedience of Christ, know with cer-
tainty, God is ready to punish all disobedience when our obedience is made complete (2 Cor. 10:1–6).

Be assured, our weapons are mighty as we pray in the power
of Christ's might (Eph. 6:10). Be confident and bold—for our
prayers, like arrows, are in the heart of the King's enemies (Ps.
45:5). Jesus Himself has gone before us; the fear of Him has the
enemy's camp in disarray.

> *Beautiful Savior, I pick up my authority, won on the
> cross, and with confidence and boldness in the One
> who saved me, I advance into the camp of the enemy
> to spread fear in the midst of battle, assured of vic-
> tory by the glorious revelation of Your fullness in my
> life! Yes and amen!*

MY SPIRITUAL PREPARATION FOR TODAY:

_____

_____

_____

TRAINED FOR WAR

*He trains my hands for war, so that my
arms bend a bow of bronze.*
—PSALM 18:34

THROUGHOUT THIS BOOK we have touched on a few of the enemies of God. It is very important to *not* charge ahead, attacking principalities and powers in spiritual warfare. The first place you need to secure is your own soul. Then, as God leads, He will give strategies that are unique to your community. He will involve a number of churches, and He will not send you out alone.

In no other dimension of life will we find the phrase "a little knowledge is a dangerous thing" more true than in spiritual warfare. It is vital that you and others in your church or community be trained in warfare before laying a large-scale siege against the enemy. Receive teaching from leaders and books, and training from Jesus our King. Step out in obedience and place your confidence securely in Him.

> *Dear Lord, I want to know You better so that I may be an effective weapon of warfare in Your hand. Please fill me with Your wisdom and discernment, and let Your presence overtake me until every bit of religion is washed from me, replaced by Your great love. I cannot do this without You. Train me and lead me in the way I should go. Thank You, Jesus. Amen.*

MY SPIRITUAL PREPARATION FOR TODAY:

_____

_____

_____

CONNECT WITH US!

CHARISMA
HOUSE

(Spiritual Growth)

f Facebook.com/CharismaHouse

y @CharismaHouse

o Instagram.com/CharismaHouseBooks

SILOAM

(Health)

p Pinterest.com/CharismaHouse

REALMS

(Fiction)

f Facebook.com/RealmsFiction